MY FATHER,
THE PRINCE

MY FATHER, THE PRINCE

THE PRINCE

Milena Petrovic-Njegoš
Thompson

To order additional copies of this book, contact:
Xlibris Corporation
1-888-7-XLIBRIS
www.Xlibris.com
Orders@Xlibris.com

Contents

TO MALCOLM

MY BELOVED HUSBAND

Preface

This is the story of the life of a man and the betrayal of a country.

Historical facts are based upon accepted publications and the reminiscences of my Father, H.H. Prince Milo of Montenegro. Some new and possibly unique perceptions of pertinent historical events and their interrelatedness as they wove the tapestry of Eastern and Southern European history in the late nineteenth and early twentieth centuries are offered for the reader's consideration.

Names of public figures have been identified correctly; however, names of certain private citizens in the Prince's personal life have been changed, and events relating thereto sometimes have been modified or altered.

The overall picture, however, is intended to accurately present Prince Milo's life's story and to give the feeling of those times, places and events that were significant to his life.

8-THOM

Personages

Montenegrin Royal House of Petrovic-Njegoš
    Prince Milo Petrovic-Njegoš, direct descendant of
        dynasty's founder, Prince Danilo I.
    Princess Milena Petrovic-Njegoš Thompson,
        daughter of Prince Milo.
    Prince-King Nicholas of Montenegro, last ruler of
        Montenegro.
    Princess-Queen Milena of Montenegro, wife of King
        Nicholas.
    Daughters of King Nicholas and Queen Milena:
        Princess Zorka, married Peter Karageorgevich
            who later became King of Serbia, mother
            of Prince Alexander, Regent of Serbia.
        Princess Militza, Grand Duchess of Russia,
            married Grand Duke Nikolai (Nikolasha,
            Nicholas) Nicolaievich.
        Princess Stana (Anastasia), Grand Duchess of
            Russia, married Grand Duke Pyotr (Pe
            -ter) Nicolaievich, brother of Grand
            Duke Nikolai.
        Princess Elena, Queen of Italy, married King
            Victor Emanuele III.
        Princess Xenia.
        Princess Anna, married Prince Franz of
            Battenberg.

Sons of King Nicholas and Queen Milena:
    Prince Danilo III.
    Prince Peter
    Prince Mirko, married Natalia
        Konstantinovich.
    Prince Michael, son of Prince Mirko and
        Princess Natalia, and grandson
        of King Nicholas.
    Helena Grace Smith Petrovic-Njegoš, married Prince
        Milo, mother of Princess Milena.

Serbian Royal House of Obrenovich.
    Prince-King Michael Obrenovich III of Serbia.
    Prince-King Milan of Serbia.
    King Alexander of Serbia, married Draga Mashin,
        Queen of Serbia.
    Queen Draga Mashin of Serbia.

Serbian Royal House of Karageorgevich.
    Prince-King Peter Karageorgevich, married Princess
        Zorka of Montenegro. Father of Regent-Prince
        Alexander.
    Regent-Prince Alexander, Son of King Peter and
        Princess Zorka, Grandson of King Nicholas and
        Queen Milena of Montenegro.

Austro-Hungarian Imperial House of Habsburg
    Emperor Franz-Josef.
    Empress Elizabeth ("Sissy"), wife of Emperor
        FranzJosef.
    Crown Prince Rudolph, Son of Emperor Franz-Josef
        and Empress Elizabeth.
    Archduke Franz-Ferdinand, Nephew of Emperor
        FranzJosef. Married Countess Sophie Chotek,
        Princess of Hohenberg, his morganatic wife.

Archduke Maximilian, Brother of Emperor Franz-
Josef, Emperor of Mexico, married Empress
Carlota, daughter of King Leopold I of Belgium.
Princess of Hohenberg, the Countess Sophie Chotek,
morganatic wife of Archduke Franz-Ferdinand.

Countess Mary Vetsera, Sweetheart of Crown Prince Rudolph.

Imperial Russia's House of Romanov
Czar Peter I, the Great.
Empress Catherine I, wife of Peter, the Great.
Empress Catherine II, the Great, wife of Czar Peter
III, the grandson of Peter, the Great.
Czar Paul I, son of Catherine, the Great.
Czar Alexander I, grandson of Catherine, the Great.
Czar Nicholas I, brother of Czar Alexander I.
Czar Alexander II, son of Nicholas I, nephew of
Alexander I.
Czar Alexander III, son of Alexander II.
Czar Nicholas II, son of Alexander III and the last
Czar of Russia. Married Empress Alexandra
Feodorovna (Princess Alix of Hesse-Darmstadt).
Children of Czar Nicholas II and Czarina Alexandra:
Czarevich Alexi
Grand Duchess Olga Nicolaievna.
Grand Duchess Tatiana Nicolaievna.
Grand Duchess Marie Nicolaievna.
Grand Duchess Anastasia Nicolaievna.
Grand Duchess Olga, sister of Czar Nicholas II.
Grand Duchess Elizabeth, sister of Czarina Alexandra.
Grand Duke Nikolai (Nicholas, Nikolasha)
Nicolaievich husband of Princess Stana
(Anastasia) of Montenegro, distant cousin of Czar
Nicholas II.
Grand Duke Pyotr Nicolaievich, brother of Grand

Duke Nikolai, married to Princess Militza of
Montenegro
Grand Duke Dimitri Pavlovich, nephew of Czar
Nicholas II.

Kaiser Wilhelm II of Germany, nephew of Czar Nicholas II.

Gregori Rasputin, a "Staret", a mystical prophet, a monk.

Alexander Kerensky, Prime Minister of Russia for half a year
between Imperial Czarism and Bolshevik Communism

Vladimir Ilyich Lenin, Leader of Communist Revolution of 1917
and Premier of the USSR.

Count Leo Tolstoy, Russian novelist and social theorist.

Leon Trotsky, Russian Commissar of War under Lenin.

Alvaro Obregon, President of Mexico.

Benito Juarez, President of Mexico.

Wallis Warfield Spencer Simpson, the Duchess of Windsor.

Edward VIII, King of England, the Duke of Windsor.

Dr. Sun Yat-sen, First President of the Republic of China after
overthrow of Manchu Dynasty.

Charlie Soong, Financial backer of Sun Yat-sen's revolution.
Daughters of Charlie Soong:
Ching-ling, married Dr. Sun Yat-sen.
May-ling, married General Chiang Kai-shek.
Ai-ling, married H.H. Kung (Kung Hsiang-hsi), di
rect descendant of Confucius.

1 | To the Emerald Isle

The road from Shannon Airport to Connemara is a long and lonely one, a three and a half to four hour drive, the Irish way, on the left side of the road. After leaving the airport I first passed through a low range of rolling green hills interspersed with a few small villages before the road led into a barren limestone plateau, a remote area unreached by the arm of civilization. The naked beauty of the rugged terrain is not without its own fascination, with a magnetic pull that is but a part of the spell that is the Emerald Isle. Even as the cold winds blowing through the Galway coast send chills reaching to the very marrow of your bones, a feeling of belonging comes over you. This seductress named Eire who has conquered many a strong and able-bodied man does not make it easy for you. But secretly she hopes you will be her match, eventually to turn and embrace her and respond to the warmth that lies beneath the surface of her wild and silent splendor.

The rocky landscape gave way to velvety green meadows dotted with white-washed thatched cottages, which then, too, retreated against another landscape, or rather rockscape, of scattered gray rocks and bleak, arid hills on which a few sheep and goats grazed lazily, as if waiting for someone to point the way to something edible. I was alone on the two-lane road leading to Errisbeg. No cars were on the horizon in any direction, nor had there been any for quite awhile. A shiver jolted me and I pressed harder on the accelerator of the Ford Escort I had rented. It seemed to be developing an extreme case of asthma which threatened to become terminal at any moment. The darkening sky with the long afternoon shadows of a late day sun set my mind to visualizing the pot of hot tea and glowing turf fire I imagined I soon would be sharing with my Father.

This was the day I had dreamed about all my life, meeting the man who was my Father, who, when I was but eight months old, had gone away, never to return.

Then my car died; just a couple of sputters with a cough-whoosh, it gave up. By now the night was almost pitch black and the few farm houses which dotted the landscape became invisible. The rain which had started a few minutes before was now coming down in torrents, blurring my vision through the windshield. It must have been over an hour since I passed the last highway sign. I felt all alone in an isolated, wet wilderness.

Reaching back to the rear seat of the car, I opened my suitcase and, fumbling around a bit, found the flashlight I had thrown in at the last moment while packing. With it I might be able to find a house where I could make a phone call to my Father so as to negate any possibly of his worrying about me. I got out of the car; and with one hand clutching my raincoat tightly around me and the other holding a rain hat in place on my head, I stalked off into the blustery winds. At first I could see no houses at all. Then I spotted a few, scattered widely apart on the stone-strewn hillside. The first one I approached showed no signs of inhabitants and there was no answer to several knocks. The second one did not have a phone. I realized then that most people out there do not have phones. I later found out that although my Father had one it usually did not work so I probably wouldn't have been able to reach him anyway.

I was now soaking-wet to the skin, hair dripping down around my face and neck, make-up vanished, and tired. The lady at the last cottage had closed the door on me very rapidly. What kind of a stranger, and a woman at that, would be out on this road at night in this kind of weather? I decided that no search-and-rescue parties would be launched before dawn, if even then. It had been a long time since stopping off at Galway for lunch and I was hungry, but the late-afternoon tea I had been dreaming of would have to remain just that.

I returned to the car. My automobile flashers probably would not last the night if left on continuously so I had better save them until I saw the headlights of a approaching car, if any ever would. I bundled myself up as best I could and settled in for a long wait, hoping someone would show up to help me but expecting to remain in an unheated car through a chilling, Irish winter night.

A half-hour to forty-five minutes must have passed before I saw the first pair of headlights in the distance, gradually becoming larger. Quickly I put on my flasher and rolled my window down a couple of inches. As it approached I saw that the vehicle was a small truck which the driver brought to a halt precisely opposite me. He rolled his window down and over the light of his dash a thin, cadaverous, male face looked squarely at me. A low-pitched voice which reminded me of Boris Karloff's at his scariest came through the howling winds.

"What's the matter? Your car broken down?"

"Yes, it is."

"Well, nothing can be done about it tonight. Where are you going? I'll give you a lift there. You can call a garage tomorrow about your car."

I asked what the nearest village was in the direction he was heading.

"But you're headed the opposite direction," he answered.

"I was headed toward Clifden, a relative lives on the way there. But you would be going in the opposite direction from the way you are traveling, so if you just take me to the next little village where there might be a room available I would be ever so appreciative."

"Here, let me get your things," he said as he got out of his truck and came toward the car. He helped me transfer my luggage from my car into his truck; and after locking my car I crawled in along side of him, keeping my thoughts to myself and hoping my trembling would appear to be from the cold and rain.

"You're turning around," I said, "I don't want you to go back as you'll be going doubly out of your way." By now he had completed his U-turn and was heading back up the road he had just traveled.

"No trouble at all, ma'am, you just let me know where to stop or turn in."

For a long time there was no conversation. After I'd had the chance to sneak a few peeks out of the corner of my eye at this stranger from the backwoods of Ireland I relaxed a bit and felt less afraid.

Then right out of the blue he asked, "Are you the daughter of that recluse prince?"

Stunned, I started to stammer, "Uh, well, yes, I guess, yes, I guess I am."

"That is the relative you are going to visit?"

"Yes."

"Well, that's easy. It's right on the road here, not far away. I'll take you directly to his house; we'll be there in about fifteen minutes. He'll be awfully happy to see you. He's waiting for you and probably worried sick about you right now."

"How do you know about me?" I inquired, rather taken back by his last remark.

"His houseman, Tom, is my best friend. I've been to your Father's place a time or two and helped out a bit. He doesn't let too many people inside the gate, a real recluse he is. That's why he's called the Recluse Prince. Tom told me you'd be coming to visit the Prince and that he was really looking forward to seeing you."

"I see." I smiled to myself and let the noise of the windshield wipers take over the conversation for awhile. The rain started letting up, and as we went over a little rise in the road we began slowing down. In the dark I could make out a gated place to my right, and we pulled to a stop in front of it.

"Here we are. I see he has his porch light on; he's obviously expecting you because it's never on. I'll get your bags out and carry them up to the house for you."

I was all aflutter. After almost forty years, for the first time in my life, I was meeting my Father. Even though the immediate circumstances seemed rather dreary, it didn't matter. It was a moment I had been waiting for, for an awfully long time.

The house sat far back from the road. Two parallel gates about ten feet apart, closed, were near the roadway. We opened the first, went through and closed it before opening the next. Within seconds the reason for the double set of gates came galloping down the driveway toward us, barking in a ferociously unfriendly manner. We both froze; I looked anxiously toward the house but my Father was nowhere in sight. Then I let out a swift, loud command, "Down!" and started walking forward, slowly. The dogs did not move nor bark. As we continued moving slowly toward the house, the dogs began to snarl. "Stop!" I called out again, "Stop!". I kept moving forward, slowly and steadily. Where was my Father, why didn't he come out?" My kind driver remained somewhat behind; I remembered he had been here before. Where was my Father?

At that moment the door to the house opened and in the doorway stood the figure of a tall, old man, framed in the light. He did not move toward us, but at this point the dogs seemed to reassess the situation. I looked around at my new friend—he gave a little smile.

"I'll leave your things at the door, ma'am, and be on my way."

He gave a nod of the head as he approached the man at the door, put my suitcases down at his side and took off his cap, giving a slight bow. With that he turned and came back down the driveway. As he stopped to say goodbye to me I tried to press a token of appreciation in his hand but he would have no part of it. It was only after he left I realized I didn't even know his name.

In that dark, cold night I stood at the foot of the steps leading

19

up to the figure that was my Father, his face still in the shadows in front of the porch light. He had not said a word. Slowly I walked up to him and put my arms around his shoulders as he put his around me. Then we drew back and looked at each other. No words passed between us; they were not necessary.

Finally, he broke the silence, "I would recognize you if I were to meet you unannounced anywhere in the world." At that we turned and went inside.

The small entry hall had been given over to the two dogs, their fluffy down beds comfortably situated on either side of the entry door. A second door led to the reception room.

"Even the dogs knew who you were. They don't obey strangers the way they did you. Amazing.!"

Upon entering the reception hall my eyes moved quickly around the room and came to rest upon the wall to my left. A life-sized oil painting of my Father in his native dress uniform, sword at his side, the tallest mountain peak of his homeland in the background, stopped my eyes from traveling any further. I stood there gazing at it in awe, completely enraptured by its beauty and majesty.

"That was a few years ago," my Father said smiling; and from the date by the artist's name I knew it was thirty five years ago that it had been painted.

"After I settled in London, around 1930, right after I left America, I was approached by this portrait artist who wanted to paint my portrait in the native costume of Montenegro, without any cost to me. All he wanted was the opportunity to show it at exhibits for a couple of years, and then it would be mine. Everywhere it went it proved to be quite an attraction. The artist received many offers from people who wanted to buy it, but he'd already promised it to me. Said that was the worst deal he'd ever made. Since then I've had numerous offers, too, but I've turned 'em all down."

"Father, please," I interrupted, "Don't ever. I hope you can understand, this is something I would treasure more than anything in the world; and I hope I am not too forward in asking now that at some future time it might come to me, irrespective of what you choose to do with anything else you have."

"It's yours, now. I shall make arrangements to have it shipped to you. It'll remind you of your old Papa when you get back home, even though that's not the way he looked when you saw him here." He chuckled, "I was sort of a handsome devil, wasn't I?"

"You sure were, and you still are." I may have stretched the point a little there at the end; the gentlemen in his eighties did look every bit his age, but the gleam in his eye and the grin on his face indicated he had lived fully every one of those years.

"I'll take you to your room. You must be very tired. Why don't you rest for awhile and then freshen up if you want to. After that I'll show you around the house so you'll know where things are, give you a bite to eat and send you off to bed for a good night's sleep. Tomorrow will be soon enough to talk."

Thus it was that H.H. Prince Milo of the Royal House of Petrovic-Njegoš of Montenegro saw his daughter for the first time since her babyhood, and vice versa. The story of his life was about to unfold.

2 | Montenegro

On October 3, 1889, in Njegusi, Montenegro, Milo, son of Djouro and Stane of the Royal House of Petrovic-Njegoš, was born. H.R.H. Prince Nicholas, ruler of Montenegro, who, later in 1910, was recrowned King Nicholas when his country became a kingdom, promptly came to visit this latest addition to his wide-flung family. Since the sixteenth century, Montenegro had been a type of theocracy wherein the country's spiritual leader, the Bishop of the Orthodox Church, was also its titular leader. The Prince-Bishop, called the Vladika, because of his religious role, was forbidden to marry. Upon his death, another unmarried, male member of the royal family, a nephew or a cousin, was chosen by election of the people to become the next Prince-Bishop. This tradition, however, was broken by Prince Danilo II, who split the two roles, retaining for himself solely the position of monarch. His successor, Prince Nicholas, married a pure-blooded Montenegrin woman named Milena Vukotich, and promptly set about making up for generations of royal, neglectful celibacy. In a twenty-five year period he sired twelve off-spring, three boys and nine girls. His own latest child, a son, Peter, had been born only five days earlier, so Nicholas was in an exceptionally joyous mood. All descendants of the family of Danilo Petrovic-Njegoš, who was the ruler in 1697 when succession became restricted to that one family, were considered part of the royal dynasty; and Nicholas paid a great deal of attention to each and every one of them. Milo had two older brothers and a sister; now together these two royal families would celebrate their latest arrivals.

Looking back years later, one could see that the years surrounding Milo's birth were a watershed for the tumultuous events that would follow during the next thirty-five years, events that would incalculably affect the lives of all members of this tiny Balkan dynasty.

In Europe, German and Austrian economic and expansionist objectives included absorbing the Balkan kingdoms into their sphere of territorial influence or control; while their rival power, Russia, promoted a Pan-Slav movement founded upon the theory that all of the Slavs of eastern Europe constituted one big, happy family. At the same time, Serbia was dreaming of extending her jurisdiction over portions of such areas as Bosnia and Herzegovina to the north-west, Croatia and Slovenia further to the north and west in the southern parts of Austria and Hungary, not to mention little Montenegro to the west. All of these precarious ambitions and schemes produced their first political fall-out on January 30, 1889, early in the same year Milo was born, when Crown Prince Rudolph of Austria, the married thirty-year old heir to the Habsburg throne, was murdered in his hunting lodge at Mayerling, sixteen miles from the Hofburg Imperial Palace in Vienna, along with seventeen-year old Baroness Mary Vetsera, his sweetheart of only two weeks. Both died of gunshot wounds, some suspected at the hands of the "Black Hand Society", a terrorist group made up of Serbian army officers. Most accounts of the incident simply crossed it off as a murder-suicide. Emperor Franz-Josef at first tried to make it appear that Rudolph had died of heart failure while Mary had taken poison (each with a gun shot wound in them?), an attempt at the proverbial government cover-up, so that suspicions would not be directed toward a country, and a man, Rudolph was known to

23

dislike: Prussia, the country; its Chancellor, Prince Otto von Bismarck, the man. The Austrian Emperor, an ally of Prussia on the surface but underneath highly suspicious and fearful of Bismarck, had taken numerous steps in the past to contain Rudolph's openly antagonistic attitude toward Germany so as to prevent Austria from finding itself on a collision course with its powerful neighbor and supposed ally. Montenegro, as well as the Slavic countries that were at that time a part of the Austrian-Hungarian Empire, were aware of the deceased Crown Prince's hostility toward Prussia and of his staunch belief in the principle of equal rights for the ethnic minorities within the Empire's borders. They had looked forward to Rudolph's ascending the Austro-Hungarian throne, and had he lived and succeeded his father, there is little doubt that the history of the Twentieth Century would have been written quite differently.

During the same year, right next door in Serbia, King Milan Obrenovich, who had ascended its throne in 1868 after his father, Prince Michael Obrenovich III, had been assassinated, after much pressure abdicated because of his continual inattention to state matters and his total ineptitude in foreign affairs. Milan's son and successor, Alexander, at that time an adolescent of thirteen, started right off developing some undesirable characteristics of his own, and within a few years time, through his Regent and advisors, instituted highly oppressive rule throughout Serbia. As a result, the kingdom's internal weaknesses multiplied, and the Austro-Hungarian Empire, with Rudolph's benevolent and moderating influence gone, quickly moved in to fill the vacuum and began exerting increasingly greater power over Serbia's foreign affairs and trade.

At the time of the assassination of Michael Obrenovich III in 1868 a peasant by the name of Marta of Kremna had forecast the extinction of the Obrenovich dynasty. Referred to as "The Black Prophecy", Milan Obrenovich had heard it but had paid it little heed. Of greater concern to him at that time was his belief that Russia had secret plans for uniting Serbia and

Montenegro, but under the latter's rule. So for the purpose of thwarting those ambitions, he had aligned his country with Austria-Hungary, thereby placing that empire in the position of being able to quickly step in and influence Serbia's policies. When it did, it did so at the cost of further alienating its own dissident Slavic minorities.

Serbia and Montenegro were settled originally by Slavic tribes that had migrated down from what is now Eastern Poland and Czechoslovakia, the original homeland of all Slavs, and adjacent Russian territories of the western Ukraine and Belorussia. In 1389, the Ottoman Turks conquered Serbia at Kosovo, the most legendary battle in Serbian history. A second defeat at

Smederevo in 1459 placed Serbia securely under Turkish military control for the next several hundred years.

Bosnia-Hercegovina and Macedonia also were overrun by the Turks. Montenegro, the most inaccessible Balkan area, north of Lake Scutari, was never subdued. It was said that Turkey once sent in an army big enough to cover all of Montenegro's tiny territory and the huge force promptly starved to death, unable to find food amid the barren cliffs and crags. Montenegrin men became famous as the best fighters in Europe. Never under foreign domination, Montenegro was always successful in fighting its enemies to maintain its freedom, only to lose it centuries later to its "friends" and allies.

In 1817 Serbia became a separate country, but still under Turkish control; in 1829 it was granted further autonomy by the Treaty of Adrianople. But it was by the Treaty of San Stefano in 1876, the document whereby the world community officially recognized Montenegro as an independent country and a princedom, that Turkey totally relinquished control of Serbia. Two years later, at the Congress of Berlin in 1878, Turkey relinquished occupation and administration of Bosnia-Hercegovina while retaining physical possession; at the same time, the "Big Powers" took the opportunity to modify the borders of both Montenegro and Serbia. During these negotiations, the Habsburg monarchy made every effort, but to no avail, to keep these two Serb countries from having common borders. Privately, she wanted to prevent any possibility of Serbia increasing her size or power. A camaraderie existed between the Emperor of Austria-Hungary and the Prince of Montenegro, not inclusive of other Slavic nations. Later, in 1906, during the reign of Peter Karageorgevich, when Austria-Hungary refused to import Serbia's main export, hogs, because Austria thought the animals were diseased, a fiasco labeled "The Pig War", the Serbians dropped the Austrians as allies in favor of France and the Russia she had previously snubbed, as those two now provided her the markets she needed.

In 1890, at age twenty-seven, Princess Zorka, the eldest

daughter of Prince Nicholas, died. For seven years she had been happily married to Peter Karageorgevich, scion of the other of Serbia's two royal dynasties and a man whom destiny would make the next King of Serbia. The betrothal of Zorka to Peter, a descendent of Serbia's peasant hero, "George the Black", had so pleased Prince Nicholas that he personally took Peter to meet Czar Alexander III of Russia, who, in turn, to show his approval of the merger of the leading families from two Balkan countries he hoped to keep under his sphere of influence, administered the wedding vows himself through the person of his Consul-General in Cetinje. All this before a crowd of Europe's finest nobility, an unusually impressive array of guests for such a small and remote country. As a wedding gift Zorka received one million rubles from the Czar.

For seven years, a princess of Montenegro and a throne-pretender to the Serbian kingdom were gloriously happy. To please her, they had settled in Cetinje near her father's residence as opposed to Belgrade, his home. But the memory of their few years together would be forever a tragically painful one for him and ever in his mind till his dying days. During a playful time together in the privacy of their bedroom she tumbled over the foot of the bed and hit her head on the floor. Soon after this accident her overall health began to deteriorate. Peter wanted to take her to the warmer climate of the Cote d'Azur or the Crimea to assist in her recovery; but Prince Nicholas, blaming Peter for her health problems, refused to issue them passports. He would later rue this day where he made the unkindest and unwisest of all his decisions, one that would ultimately lead to his personal downfall and the demise of his country. Years later there were those who commented that Nicholas should never have let Zorka marry a Karageorgevich; what he should never have done was to interfere in the affairs of a happily married couple. A country would topple because of it—his. Instead, his daughter, had she lived, would have become the Queen of Serbia.

Her death was a blow to both of them; each in his own way

loved her very much. Bitter about his former father-in-law, Peter left Montenegro with his three surviving children from Zorka's five pregnancies, for Geneva, Switzerland, to start a new life. Completely on his own now, in order to make ends meet he took a job as a bookkeeper in a small hotel and then later became a legal translator, his love for Zorka never wavering. His own place in the sun was yet to come.

Milo's early years developed against this backdrop of an increasingly unrestful Balkan canvas. He grew into a handsome youth in his tiny hometown of Njegusi, not far from the capital of Cetinje, up a treacherous, hair-pin curving, mountainous road. Story goes that the highway engineer of the road fell in love with Princess Milena and made a special "M" curve in the road in her honor. Ostensibly, the Princess said nothing, but Prince Nicholas saw to it that the man was punished severely. Njegusi lies in a fertile valley at the foot of Mt. Lovcen, (the famed "Black Mountain"), at the top of which is the white stone mausoleum containing the remains of Peter II, the Prince-Bishop who became one of the South Slavs greatest poets.

Looking much the same today as they did then, the homes were built of stone, low and unpretentious. One house was a combined school and telegraph office for the town and neighboring community. Less than an hour away was Cetinje, called the smallest capital in the world. No imposing buildings there either, no traffic, more of a village or township than a city, consisting of one broad street lined with two-story houses, the King's palace being identifiable only because it was the largest one, and a large market-square. Actually the finest buildings in Cetinje were the foreign embassies, practically every country had one there, the Russian and Austrian ones being the largest and most imposing. Close by were a tiny theatre where Nicholas' plays were produced, his most famous being "Empress of the Balkans", a small hospital, and a co-educational high school. There were no shops as we know them, not a large plate of glass for a store front anywhere. Merchandise was displayed on the floor or on the walls of the front room of any house, the shopkeeper packing a fully-loaded revolver in his belt or sash. A loaded revolver was worn at all times by men, prince and peasant alike—this was the law of the land; women often wore one, too. It's rough country here, this land of naked rock and jagged mountains and valleys that look like the craters of extinct volcanoes. The people that took to this lofty and isolated spot centuries ago were refugees from fierce battles and brutal savagery. Survival occurred only due to acts of unmatched bravery. The history of Montenegro is a continuous record of heroic deeds in a centuries-old struggle with the Turks in defense of freedom, faith and home.

1893 brought cause for great celebration to this modest princedom. It was the 400th anniversary of Montenegro having possessed the Balkans' first printing press, the first printing press among all the Slav countries, and the printing of the first Slavic book, the "Oktoih", the service book of the Orthodox Church. Almost every country in the world sent a representative to this auspicious occasion. For four-year old Milo this was his first taste of international excitement, seeing the visitors from the foreign countries in their widely varied national garb, listening to the sounds of speech so very different from his own.

During the ceremony, the representative from the University of Oxford was quoted as saying, "This nation of heroes was able to print its works in its native tongue at a time when, as yet, Oxford had no printing press of its own."

Prime Minister William Gladstone of England sent his deputy to read his statement, "This printing press made its appearance seven years after that of London, when neither Oxford, Cambridge nor Edinburgh possessed one. It was not until sixteen years later that the first printing press was established in Rome, the capital of Christendom, and it was twenty-eight years after that that the first book was published there."

The Academy of Sciences of St. Petersburg sent a message which properly reflected the character of the little nation, which included the following statement:

"This indestructible rampart, Montenegro, has made its presence felt not only by its heroic deeds but also by its civilizing influence."

The country basked in the glory of the acclaim it was receiving for its attention to the mind as well as to the sword. However, the royal family's cultural tendencies had displayed themselves some years earlier, at the opposite end of the continuum, when in 1865 the first pool table was brought to Montenegro! (To this day they probably don't have too many more.) It arrived by boat at the harbor and had to be carried up to the palace by mule!

It was Easter, 1897, the year of the bicentenary of the Petrovic-Njegoš dynasty. Milo's family was invited to join in the dual celebrations by spending a few days at the Royal Palace in Cetinje. Early morning sun colors bleached the mountains in the background with a golden hue as communal sheep and goats grazed in pastures dry and parched, while higher up in the mountains, wolf and wild boar roamed freely among the pine and beech trees. A young girl's voice could be heard singing as she led her donkey up a trail with a load of kindling wood. During the Lenten fast, which was very strict in the Eastern Orthodox Church, one partook of no meat, fish, cheese, nor eggs; nothing but bread and parboiled beans for the faithful. A few days before Easter Sunday, the housewives would begin preparing their famous Easter eggs. First boiled with logwood, or cochineal, or aniline dye, sometimes wrapped in onion skins before boiling so as to achieve a mottled brown, tortoise shell-like appearance, the eggs were then given to the egg artists who, with a very fine brush or feather, drew the beautiful traditional patterns on them while at the same time making them look as if they were covered with crimson lace.

Before the time of Christ, the exchanging of Easter eggs was the symbol of life renewing itself in the springtime; in the Christian era the Easter egg became the emblem of the Resurrection of Christ. In the Near East, even today, one may see in some dim-lit church, on the walls of which loom weird figures of Byzantine saints, numerous ostrich eggs hanging near the altar.

Nine-year old Milo liked it when his parents brought him and his brothers and sister to Cetinje. Wide-eyed and fascinated by all this, he excitedly joined in with the groups of eager, hungry children rushing up to the grown-ups in hopes of being rewarded with an egg. The recipient of an egg brandished it high in the air and challenged anyone else with an egg to fight him. When another child accepted the challenge, they tapped their eggs together. The egg that cracked was the vanquished one and had to be handed over to the victor. The streets became crimson with eggshells. It was then a point of honor to eat all the eggs you won. Milo won many and he ate many and quite a few children, including Milo, were not well the next day.

A shot rang through the air and church bells began to chime, announcing the arrival of Prince Nikita as his subjects loved to call him. Emerging from the Palace, he strode across the broad street to greet his officers, forty in number, lined up in full dress for his inspection. One of the many unusual facets of Montenegrin life even today is the beauty and brilliance of their everyday clothing. Only slightly more extravagantly dressed than his people, the Prince, his large frame always a flamboyant figure, was a magnificent sight in a full-skirted, long white coat shaped in at the waist and decorated with gold braided embroidery; a heavy, multi-colored silk sash over blue breeches set off his high Russian boots of soft, black leather. Stuck in the sash around his waist was the perennial revolver, and upon his head he wore the "Kapa", a small, round, black hat with a red crown, in the Prince's case made of velvet, to signify the blood shed in battle upon the rough rocks of Montenegro. Five gold circles were embroidered on the crown, each symbolizing one hundred years of fighting. In the center of the Prince's crown were the letters, H.I., the Greek form of Nicholas I. Women's everyday dress was similar to the men's long coats and sashes, but over long skirts. At all times the country displayed a very colorful and festive appearance.

After Nikita walked down the line of officers, greeting every man with a kiss on each cheek, he moved away, taking Milo with him, to sit under a large elm tree, his daily custom, weather permitting, holiday or not. The people were now free to come and visit with the Prince. He knew most of his subjects by name. Many just came to chat, others to inquire about news of other countries, while some sought advice about their farms. People also asked him to settle their disputes and arguments. There was so little crime in the country there were no courts. But Nicholas was already planning ahead and by 1905 he had developed a constitution for the country and had established courts of law. From that point on, the people took their disputes to the court, and the Prince sat under the elm tree no more. Old customs die hard; the people had wanted a constitution and courts of law and now they had them, but they had lost something in the process.

Off to one side a minstrel played his gusle, a violin-like instrument with one string and a cross-bow. People listened as he sang about the glory of Crna Gora (Montenegro) and its heroes. After he finished, the men started to dance a slow and stately dance called the "Kolo", all singing together. Women were noticeable by their absence; throughout the entire celebration, they remained in their houses, another custom in this Land of the Black Mountain.

Nikita walked back to the Palace with Milo at his side. He liked this young boy and wanted to begin planning for the youth's future.

In Austria-Hungary, 1898 was the year of the Golden Jubilee, the 50th anniversary of the reign of Emperor Franz-Josef. Empress Elizabeth, "Sissy" as he used to call her, was away from Vienna much of the time. Ever since Rudolph's death, the Empress wore mourning and kept in seclusion, sometimes in Lainz near Vienna, other times in Godollo near Budapest; now she had just completed a month at the spa at Bad Nauheim for an assortment of ailments and had gone to recuperate at Caux, Switzerland, a spot with gorgeous views of Lake Geneva and the surrounding Alps. She wrote her husband frequently, telling him how happy she was there and asking him to join her, but the old Emperor really had no choice but to refuse, what with all the extra Jubilee festivities on top of his regular commitments. The Viennese actress, Katherine Schratt, whom he had met through "Sissy", offered him companionship whenever the Empress chose to be away. The actress had bought a residence next to Schonbrunn Palace and a villa in Bad Ischl, the Emperor's "get away" retreat. She also rented an apartment near the Hofburg, the main palace in the heart of Vienna, which, of course, was near a number of theatres in which she performed. A beloved friend, the Emperor, nonetheless, never stopped loving his "Sissy".

After a delightful visit the afternoon of May 9th with her friend, the Baroness de Rothschild, at her estate near Geneva, Empress Elizabeth spent the night at the Hotel Beau Rivage prior to returning the next day to Caux. She and her lady-in-waiting, Countess Sztaray, visited a music store in the morning, allowing just enough time to catch the afternoon boat to Territet, the port for Caux. As she was walking toward the Quai Mt. Blanc to board the lake steamer, a young Italian anarchist, Luigi Lucheni, pushing aside her lady-in-waiting, darted in front of the Empress. He peered beneath her parasol to make certain of her identity, then plunged a dagger into her chest. As quickly as he appeared, he disappeared. Elizabeth fell to the ground with not a sound.

As the countess helped Elizabeth to her feet, others came running to see if she were injured and to try to help. As they dusted off her clothes, she said it was nothing and with normal steps continued on and walked up the gangplank of the steamer. At the top, she collapsed on the deck. Efforts to revive the Empress were unsuccessful. As Countess Sztaray opened her bodice to allow for easier breathing, she screamed. Blood oozed from a wound above Elizabeth's left breast. She was carried on a stretcher back to the hotel and minutes later, after the doctors' efforts to revive her failed, she passed away.

Franz-Josef was sixty-eight, and this assassination was almost more than he could bear, the third violent death in the immediate family. First, his brother, Emperor Maximilian of Mexico, executed by direction of Benito Juarez before a revolutionary firing squad; second, his son, Crown Prince Rudolph of Austria shot at Mayerling; and now, during the year of his Golden Jubilee, his beloved wife, Elizabeth, knifed to death in Geneva. For awhile it appeared as if this tragedy might unite the peoples of central Europe; mourning was universal and genuine. But that was not to be.

Archduke Franz-Ferdinand, nephew of the Emperor and now heir to the Habsburg empire, had already met and was in love with a lovely German countess, Sophie Chotek, of Chotkova and Wogin (Czechoslovakia), but was keeping it secret from the high society of the royal court. Since the death of Elizabeth, he had taken greater interest and had become more active in the affairs of state and, as a result, became quite concerned about the agitations of the southern Slavs within the Empire. A quick trip down the Dalmatian coast in 1899 convinced him of the necessity for a new policy designed to accommodate the needs and wishes of increasingly vocal nationalistic groups, just as had the assassinated Crown-Prince Rudolph before him. But, just as he had previously ignored Rudolph' opinions, the old Emperor paid no attention to Franz-Ferdinand's report; he was more focused on opposing his nephew's marriage to the Countess Sophie. Even though she was the daughter of a diplomat of old lineage, the Emperor considered her a woman of too low a rank to marry the heir to the throne. By accepting a position for a short period of time as lady-in-waiting to the Archduchess Isabella, wife of a distant relative within the royal family, so as to be close to Franz-Ferdinand, Sophie had unintentionally cemented Franz-Josef's attitude. However, the Emperor finally broke down and gave his permission for the marriage, but only under the condition that it be a morganatic one, wherein the spouse of lower status does not share the rank of the higher born. None of the children of this union could succeed to the crown. Sophie would receive none of the rights, trappings, coats of arms, or privileges of the royal family. In state processions she would forever walk behind even the youngest Archduchesses. It was this or lose his beloved. So he agreed.

On June 23, 1900, at Schonbrunn Palace, Franz-Ferdinand signed the renunciation barring any of his possible progeny from succession to the throne. Five days later, on June 28th, the renunciation was repeated in a solemn, public ceremony at high noon at the Hofburg Palace before all the highest notables of Austria. As a minor token of appeasement, the Emperor promised Sophie the title of Princess upon her marriage even though she would never be a true member of the House of Habsburg. It would be fourteen years, to the very same hour, on the very same day of the very same month, that two shots would ring out in a city called Sarajevo.

Prince Nicholas and Princess Milena of Montenegro were invited to the wedding, a small one by royal standards, and one many of the higher Austrian nobility had been discouraged from attending. But FranzFerdinand's rapport with many of the Southern Slavs brought all of those invited to Vienna for the nuptial day. The Prince and Princess decided to bring Milo, now eleven years old, his first trip to the beautiful Austrian capital. Arriving in Vienna June 30th, the evening before the wedding, there being no pre-wedding festivities for the betrothed couple except for a Saturday night intimate dinner, Nicholas, Milena and Milo went straight to the Hotel Imperial, official host then, and still to this day, to Europe's royalty and visitors of state from around the world. Built in 1867 as the palatial home of the Duke of Wurttemberg, it was transformed into a hotel a few years later, retaining all its original elegant opulence and dignity.

July 1st was a gray and dismal wedding morning. Rain fell on the roof of the Hofburg Palace in seeming dreary accompaniment to the tolling of the bells in the church steeple. The ceremony was set for eleven in the morning in the chapel at the palace, not at Vienna's grand St. Stephen's Cathedral. Most of the guests were close relatives and friends who cared more for the couple than for the posturing of the Emperor. As the organ prelude sounded, the bride, attended by Princess Lowenstein, walked down the aisle to the palm-decked altar with six-foot candles burning on each side, beautiful in a gown of white satin, behind which swept a pearl-encrusted seven-foot train. On her head she wore a simple myrtle wreath and veil, while around her neck and on her earlobes a diamond necklace and earrings. Myrtle and lillies of the valley, favorites of the murdered Empress Elizabeth, comprised her bouquet. Franz-Ferdinand stood at the altar wearing the Golden Fleece and Grand Cross of the Order of St. Stephen on his general's dress cavalry uniform. Milo took special note of this, as he had already made up his mind he wanted to be the commander of the Montenegrin cavalry. Franz-Ferdinand was attended by his good friend, the Count Nostitz, while the dean of the castle chapel, not the Archbishop of Vienna, performed the ceremony.

Later, during the wedding dinner at the castle, true to his promise, Emperor Franz-Josef pronounced Sophie Princess of Hohenberg, with the title, "Her Grace". To the strains of the Imperial anthem, perhaps the only indication that this was a marriage of the heir to the throne, little else reflecting that fact, the couple left on their honeymoon for Konopischt. To young Milo, however, it was all overwhelmingly impressive.

After spending a few days at a spa on the outskirts of Vienna, the Prince and Princess of Montenegro, with Milo in tow, returned home by way of England, where they were to visit the Queen. Milo was soon to have something to really impress him. When the train pulled into the London station from Southhampton, there to greet them in person was Queen Victoria herself, an honor she rarely bestowed.

Those few days in London were like a dream. His life in little Montenegro could hardly compare with what he was experiencing now, dinner at Windsor Castle where the Prince and Princess of Montenegro were the guests of honor, and in a way, so was he. The magnificence and vastness of the castle compared with the simplicity and smallness of the palace at Cetinje brought new dimensions to his world, as had the recently completed visit to Vienna. He began to respect the many things Nicholas had instituted in Montenegro; pride and loyalty began growing in his heart for the little country which was hardly a spot on the map. He knew then he would spend the rest of his life trying to help his country, just as Queen Victoria had helped hers. One year later the Victorian era passed into history. In January of 1901, she died.

While Franz-Ferdinand and Sophie had shaken up court circles with their marriage, to the south, the former teenager who became King of Serbia, Alexander Obrenovich, announced his engagement to Draga Mashin, a beautiful widow ten years his senior, who had first been his mistress, and prior to that, the mistress of many of the men in the Serbian Officers Corps. It was widely circulated that she was infertile and would be unable to bear Alexander any heirs. Efforts to sidetrack this unpopular union by introducing Alexander to the also beautiful and still unmarried Princess Xenia of Montenegro were to no avail. Had the romance blossomed, a second Montenegrin princess would have become a member of the other Serbian royal dynasty, the Obrenoviches, and as a result, Queen of Serbia. Against the tide of public opinion throughout Serbia, King Alexander married Draga Mashin in the summer of 1900, and the former acknowledged whore of practically the entire political and military elite became Queen of Serbia. The cabinet resigned. No one was willing to form a new government but Alexander showed no regrets. Fierce national pride found this marriage intolerable and three years later doomed it to a tragic end.

Meanwhile, right next door, in 1902, one of Prince Nicholas' three sons, Prince Mirko, took a beautiful Montenegrin, Natalia Konstantinovich, as his bride, and happily five children were born of this alliance, the only grandchildren old Nicholas would have from his three sons. One, Michael, as the grandson of Montenegro's last ruler, years later during World War II, would be presented with an appalling proposal, which, upon his rejection, would then be extended to Milo.

In 1903 a faction of Serbia's military began planning a coup d'etat to force the abdication of King Alexander and his Queen Draga, with plans for worse if he were to refuse. Prince Peter Karageorgevich, now a sixty-year old man, still living quietly in Geneva, had been contacted regarding accepting the crown of Serbia. If a peaceful transition could be accomplished he would accept, he said, but he made it clear he wanted no violence. However, Peter understood all too well that a new king acceptable to the people, as he would be, was absolutely essential if Serbia was to avoid a revolution or if the country were to avoid being taken over by Austria-Hungary to the north or, he thought, even Montenegro to the west. Prince Nicholas, he felt, wouldn't mind at all moving in at a moment of Serbian weakness, as he had once spoken of a union of Southern Slavs under his rule. If Peter refused to return to Serbia, sooner or later Serbia's crown might belong to Prince Nicholas; Peter's last days in Montenegro with Nicholas' own daughter dying in his arms after Nicholas denying them exit visas remained stuck in his craw. He would do anything to deny Prince Nicholas his pleasure.

Prince Nicholas had become a central figure in the royal diplomacy of southern Europe; due to the marriages of his daughters he had gained the nickname of "the father-in-law" of Europe. In addition to Zorka's marriage to Peter, now becoming the King of Serbia; Elena had become the Queen of Italy by her marriage to Victor Emanuele III; Militza married Grand Duke Pyotr (Peter) Nicolaievich of Russia and Stana (Anastasia) married Grand Duke Nikolai (Nicholas, Nikolasha) Nicolaievich of Russia; while Anna married Prince Franz-Josef of Battenberg. A visitor, while flattering Nicholas as the modernizer of Montenegro, expressed regret that the country had no exports, received the jovial reply, "Ah, but you forget my daughters." All of this had bestowed upon the Prince of Montenegro a considerable amount of clout and prestige and more than once the fear had been raised that he, too, harbored secret ambitions that also went beyond the borders of his own country.

The land of conspiracies, suspicions, and brutality once again was about to live up to its reputation. Their lusts now unfulfilled, all of the officers who had formerly received Draga's favors were out to extract their revenge. Their leader, Colonel Mashin, the brother of her deceased first husband, had carried a fierce hatred for her ever since being involuntarily retired by King Alexander soon after the marriage; and he was out to square the account.

On the night of June 10, 1903, in downtown Belgrade, as the clock struck midnight, a group of about thirty or forty loud, drunken officers cavorted around on a side street to the sounds of gypsy music being poured forth by a group of local musicians. When the captain of the officers called out, "Stop, we go now," the street was suddenly deserted by all except this group of aroused fanatics searching for old wine and new blood. They knew where they were going; they headed straight for the royal palace.

As they approached the palace, without solicitation the gates opened; and the wild insurrectionists, eager to carry out their fiendish plans, quickly found their way upstairs to the royal bedroom where the gruesomely unthinkable became the hideous reality. Only a few words passed between the officers and the King and Queen before a shot rang out and Alexander slipped to the floor. As Draga grasped for her wounded husband, a sword flashed through the air and ran across her abdomen, cutting off her left breast. The King and Queen of Serbia were kicked, stomped upon, crushed; and after the soldiers satisfied themselves that the two victims were indeed dead, they began looting and helping themselves to anything and everything in sight. Lastly, the bodies were defenestrated. First the Queen's nude body was thrown out the window, landing spread-eagled on the ground at the feet of waiting soldiers. A minute later the sound of bones cracking as they it hit the hard surface below registered the second body landing in front of a now cheering crowd.

Cries of "Long live King Peter" filled the air. Marta of Kremna's "Black Prophecy" had been fulfilled. It was a new day for Serbia; and the man that Prince Nicholas of Montenegro had first befriended and made his son-in-law, and then offended and made his enemy, was now King of the neighboring Serb country many times larger and many times stronger than his. Had she lived, Zorka, the Prince of Montenegro's own daughter, would now have been its Queen.

Imagine how different the history of the Balkans would have been if either of the Montenegrin princesses had become Queen of Serbia! Or if, in turn, both had!

3 | St. Petersburg

In 1902, twelve year old Prince Milo was sent to St. Petersburg, Russia, to spend the next seven years of his life at the elite Corps des Pages Military Academy, for five years of general education followed by two years of specialization, in his case in cavalry training, preparing him for entry into the officers' ranks of the Montenegrin army. Throughout all of Europe, sons of the leading families of royalty and nobility were signed up, as early as at birth, in order to be eligible to apply for admission to the famous military school; to be even considered, a potential student had to be from a noble family with military connections and impeccable credentials.

Russia entered the Twentieth Century having changed very little over the past few hundred years. She retained her position as the grand monarchy of the later seventeenth-century style, displaying a veneer of mystical Imperialism superimposed over a structure of coarse barbarianism not far beneath the surface. Illiterate peasant life revolved around religious beliefs founded upon Christian ideology and a reverence for the monarchy grounded on a naive assumption that the monarch and his noble men were good and would do whatever was best for the people. At the court level, Czar Nicholas II's international policies were completely manipulated by his wily cousin, Kaiser Wilhelm II of Germany, who was desirous of diminishing Russia's influence in Europe, and in line with that aim, encouraged the Czar to pursue an aggressive foreign policy in the Far East. The Russian masses were not aware of any of this. Russia had completed the Trans-Siberian Railroad and she had received approval from China for a connecting line on to Port Arthur at the Yellow Sea. The Czar's fantasies for expansion in the Far East constantly being aroused, Russia then applied pressure on China to grant them a ninety-nine year lease on the port. Ever prodded on by the German Kaiser, Russia decided to invade Korea. However, they made the mistake of not taking one thing into proper account, the rising power of Japan. Unwisely, they ignored the efforts of the highest ranking Japanese statesmen who tried to head off what was developing into a hostile situation.

During all this time enormous changes in thinking were taking place among all classes of Russian citizens. Intolerance of social injustices began building in the minds of the masses: the peasantry, the intelligentsia, the industrialists, the students, some minority nationalities, the Jews, even among some of the landowners. New philosophies were taking shape; and the process of the politicalization of the working class, which had begun some years prior, was rapidly escalating. There was no middle class, no widely diffused broad education capable of mitigating overemotional reactions to crises. The country moved into a time of unrest, a time for demonstrations. There were massive peasant disorders in central Russia; strikes that originated in the oil-producing city of Baku on the Caspian Sea spread all across southern Russia. The universities became the internal breeding ground for revolutionaries, while on the outside police intervention against two radical groups, the Social Democrats and the full-fledged Marxists, became ever stronger and more frequent. As leaders of some of these new revolutionary philosophies and critics of the status quo were arrested and exiled to Siberia for varying periods of time, underground revolutionary centers sprung up to take their place. Because government restrictions were minimal and police supervision sloppy, the exiles took this as a golden opportunity to read, write, study and plan their future activities. In Geneva, Switzerland, an exile by the name of Vladimir Ilyich Lenin was busy developing the party and underground organization that would wage and win the socialistic revolution that was to come. All the revolutionaries that had become prominent and outspoken during this time were so preoccupied with their own internal squabbles for power and jockeying for position that they failed to concern themselves with the possibility of a war with Japan or what it might mean to them. During this time the Czar seemed unaware or disinterested in what was happening to his empire, domestically or internationally. An impending avalanche of destruction was slowly building a climax. An entire civilization was soon to be completely pulled up from its roots.

Milo's trip to Russia to commence his education there, coming as it did at what would later prove to be a most extraordinary period of time in world history, offered Prince Nicholas a good excuse to visit the young Czar Nicholas II and the Czarina Alexandra Feodorovna, who had been Queen Victoria's favorite granddaughter, and learn first-hand about what was going on. The Czar's grandfather, Czar Alexander II, had been the Godfather of one of Nicholas' daughters, Princess Elena, now the Queen of Italy.

Joyously greeting Nicholas and Milo at the St. Petersburg train station were Prince Nicholas' two daughters and their brother husbands, Grand Duke Nikolai (Nicholas, Nikolasha) Nicolaievich, and Grand Duchess Princess Stana (Anastasia), who had divorced her first husband, the Duke of Leuchtenberg, to marry Nikolai; and Grand Duke Pyotr (Peter) Nicolaievich and Grand Duchess Princess Militza. In their two landaus they transported the new arrivals to the Hotel de l'Europe (the Europa) on the fashionable Nevsky Prospekt, the main street of the city; "Toleration Street" it was sometimes referred to because of the many churches of different faiths built on it. Awaiting the arrival of His Royal Highness at the hotel was a courier from the Imperial Court, with a letter in French, the language used by the Court, from the Czar, through his secretary. His Imperial Majesty was at Peterhof Palace (Petrodvorets), just a few miles from St. Petersburg proper, for only a couple of weeks, on his way from his yearly August retreat at his hunting lodge in Poland to the Crimea where he spent each September and March. The letter read:

> The Imperial Palace
> The Village of Peterhof
> Grand Marshalate of the Imperial Court
> September 2, 1902
> Your Royal Highness,
>
> I am commanded by His Imperial Majesty, the Emperor of All the Russias, to express to you His Imperial Majesty's pleasure at your arrival in St. Petersburg. His Imperial Majesty, the Emperor, and Her Imperial Majesty, the Empress, request your presence to dinner at this palace at six o'clock. His Excellency, the Minister of Transportation, has placed at your disposal a carriage for your use during your entire stay. The officer who conveys this letter to you will serve as your personal guide during this time.
>
> Accept, Your Royal Highness, the assurances of my highest esteem.
>
> Gavril, Grand Marshall

Upon expressing his acceptance of the invitation to the courier, an unnecessary action as it would be expected, Nicholas turned to his daughters and said, "We'll see you there, of course. Hopefully we shall all sit together; I see you so infrequently now that your home is St. Petersburg that while I'm here I hope to spend as much time with you as possible."

"Oh, we will, Daddy, don't you worry. We also want to show Milo around a bit before he starts school and gets all encompassed with his studies. Our old school, the Smolny (educational institute established by Catherine II for daughters from noble families of Europe), has girls from more countries than ever this year. We are often asked to serve as hostesses at the palace when they are brought over to see it and to meet the Czarina. It's part of their education. Milo is so tall and handsome, I am sure some of the pretty young countesses or baronesses attending the Smolny will take good note of him." Milo hadn't begun yet to think about girls and blushed at Stana's remark.

Promptly at five o'clock that evening, Prince Nicholas and Prince Milo, bedecked in very finest national costumes of Montenegro, with all appurtenant medals and ribbons appended thereon, departed the Europa Hotel in an elegant carriage with two fine horses and a pigtailed and powdered coachman sitting in the driver's seat (quite beyond the customary attire of the regular izvoshniki, or cab man). Footmen, similarly dressed, who had stood by the horses and at the carriage door as the royal guests entered, leaped up, one beside the coachman and the other in back, for the trip to the palace at Peterhof.

Situated on the Neva river and spread across nineteen main islands and hundreds of small ones, with sixty-six rivers and veinous canals connected by some six hundred bridges, St. Petersburg was the creation of one mind, that of Peter the Great. It grew out of a total concept of its founder, not piece-meal, in that Peter wanted to introduce and implant Western European civilization in Russia, as well as have a port city facing west so as to maintain the cultural and commercial contact with North and Western Europe he so studiously developed and admired. Designed and constructed on a vast scale by European architects, with wide spaces and enormous structures, the city reflects a predominately Italian flavor on the outside and with increasing

45

French influences on the inside. The Cathedral of Our Lady of Kazan, for example, was built as a direct copy of St. Peter's Basilica in Rome.

As they pulled out onto the Nevsky Prospekt Milo marveled at the resplendent, beautiful main street of the then capital of Russia. Facades of brightly lit shop windows were painted with pictures of the merchandise offered for sale inside. They passed the "Gostinni Dvor", a covered Westernized version of an Eastern bazaar, a Merchants' Row with open market trading in front, while immediately past it was an elegant hairdresser, with wigs on display and separate entrances for ladies and gentlemen. For three miles along the southern bank of the Neva ran the gold, blue and white Winter Palace and Hermitage Museum, the gold-spired Admiralty Museum, the foreign embassies and palaces of other royalty and nobility. The pavement was spotlessly clean. People were out walking, men in long frock-coats with their ladies in beautifully hued redingotes and coordinating hats, French-style lampposts illuminating the way in the not-yet-darkening late afternoon. It was considered the most elegant city in the world; and even with all the wars and revolutions that have engulfed it since, it still is.

The ride to Peterhof took them through some very pretty countryside, quite English in style, with alternating vistas of green islands, green grass and green, wooded trees, with numerous smaller palaces interspersed in amongst. White marble statues and graceful fountains tossing jets of water at the sky came into view as part of the Imperial Park; the illumination of the trees making the leaves appear as diamonds. The driver of the carriage announced that two hundred and fifty thousand lamps were blazing, the fire of which shed an artificial light far exceeding that of a regular northern day. Eighteen hundred men were required to light them all within an allotted thirty-five minute period. Though it was still daylight and would be for about four more hours, through the "white nights" thousands of people were sauntering around in the park: soldiers, tradesmen, lords, peasants, all quietly and respectfully admiring and enjoying the beauty around them.

In front of the carriage a space opened up and there before them loomed Peterhof Palace. Foaming cascades of water rushed down in two wide arms of six colored marble steps into a large basin and from this into a long canal flanked by rows of trees, statuary and fountains leading through the lower gardens to the Neva Bay below. Frequently referred to as "the Versailles de la mer", now called Petrodvorets, Peterhof Palace was built by Peter, the Great, in 1715, just ten years before he died. Later reconstructed by his daughter, Empress Elizabeth, it stands on a natural slope of ground that slants down toward Neva Bay with a panoramic view across the Gulf to the Finnish Coast. Splendor beyond comprehension left Milo stunned.

As the carriage pulled up at the entrance to the salute of two rows of guards, a white powdered footman came forward to open the carriage doors. Upon alighting, the two were led up a flight of steps to a grand entry foyer. As servants came forward to take their coats, a pair of folding doors beyond swung open and a properly powdered and dignified official in crimson jacket with lace, carrying a gold and ebony stave, swished through to greet them.

"Your Royal Highness, Your Highness, in the name of His Imperial Majesty, The Czar, and Her Imperial Majesty, the Czarina, I welcome you. I am Gavril, at your service. Please follow me."

Walking through a second marble entry salon filled with huge oil paintings and life-sized statues, they were led on to another pair of doors that opened into a long hall, richly carpeted in blue and gold, each wall flanked with somewhat smaller but equally priceless paintings. At the far end were two more footmen making ready to open still a third pair of doors as they approached. They entered a vast room with a lofty ceiling soaring into a dome far above their heads, filled with such a crowd of people they could hardly move, in groups, talking and laughing, the men in uniforms of all colors of the rainbow, the women in full-skirted

47

satin and lace dresses with plumes and trains, and fabulous jewels on their ears, around the necks, and on their arms and fingers, to dazzle even the most jaded of the nobility. Obviously this was to be an evening more gala than they had anticipated.

The first group opened their ranks to admit Gavril and Nicholas and Milo.

"I have the honor to present His Royal Highness, the Prince of Montenegro, and His Highness, Prince Milo of Montenegro. Your Royal Highness, Your Highness, I present to you the Grand Duke Dimitri Pavlovich, Baron and Baroness Yuri Nervsky, the Grand Duke Ivann Konstantinovich, the Grand Duchess, Princess Yelena Petrovna and her niece, Countess Irena Vladmir."

Gavril completed his introductions just in time as an assistant was at his elbow to whisper something in his ear. "Excuse me, please, Your Royal Highness, Your Highness, Your Excellencies. I must take leave for a little while. Please forgive me." Bowing, he backed out of the group and disappeared into the crowd.

The Emperor and Empress came into view as they made their way through the roomful of guests, responding to the deep bows and curtsies with a nod, opting for a few remarks with chosen guests. Marshall Gavril was at the Czar's side, doing the necessary introductions of any persons Their Imperial Majesties might not have previously met personally, but as Emperor Nicholas II's eye caught that of Prince Nicholas he gave a broad smile and moved forward to greet the older monarch of the little Balkan country.

"Your Royal Highness, it pleased us greatly to hear you had come to St. Petersburg again, this time to place your cousin at the Corps des Pages. And is this the young man?"

"Yes, Your Majesty," responded Prince Nicholas. "Permit me to present to you Prince Milo of the dynasty of Petrovic-Njegoš."

Milo clicked his heels and bowed. "I am honored, Your Majesty".

"During the time you are at the academy here in St. Petersburg

I shall look forward to seeing you a number of times; you will be hearing from me," the Russian monarch smiled at Milo, and continued with a twinkle in his eye, "Milo, I want you to keep a good eye on your cousin here this evening; we have a surprise for him and we want to be sure he remains wide awake for it!"

"I shall be certain to do that, Your Majesty."

As Their Imperial Majesties moved on, Nicholas began looking around the room for sight of his two daughters while Milo observed a double line of soldiers filing into the room, tall young men in breast-plates of highly polished silver, silver helmets to match with white plumes waving in the air.

"That is the Chevalier Guard, all young men of noble birth," explained the very young Countess Irena, of an age most certainly close to Milo's.

She looked at them approvingly, huge, handsome men picked for their height and appearance, which Milo found pleased him, yet somehow, at the same time, slightly distressed him. During his time in St. Petersburg when he would not be required to be at the Corps des Pages he had been invited to participate in the Chevalier Guard, an honor not frequently granted a non-Russian nobleman. He watched carefully as the guardsmen took their assigned places against the walls, two or three yards apart, each standing erect like a silver statue as he reached his post. Soon he would be doing this. From Alexander I to the 6'5" Alexander III, the Russian monarchy was made up of giant men of Slavic heritage, just like the Montenegrin royalty. Milo already had reached 6' and would add another 3" before returning home. The accession of Nicholas II brought to the throne a slender, 5' 7" man, displaying the hereditary results of recent marriages of Romanovs to non-Russian, Northern Europeans, who were relatively small in comparison to their Slavic counterparts. The Romanovs were decreasing in stature, in more ways than one, as history would bear out.

Focusing his attention back on the entire room Milo observed the people moving slowly away from the center, thereby permitting

49

the royal family to walk down the middle to take specially positioned seats, the Czar and Czarina in ornate armchairs, the princes and princesses in upright gold-leaf and satin cushioned chairs. As people walked around they were careful not to commit the most horrible of breaches of etiquette, that of having one's back to the royalty.

"Papa, here we are." Stana and Militza and their husbands were at Nicholas' side. After doing the introductions to the recent acquaintances, Nicholas' expression caused all eyes to follow the direction of his, to see that a beautiful buffet table had quietly been rolled in. The guests were starting to wend their way in that direction, and the young Countess spoke up.

"Your Royal Highness," she said, addressing her remark to Prince Nicholas. "Would you and Their Highnesses care to follow me over to the buffet? I am sure you will find appetizers pleasing to your taste."

"Oh, I am most certain we will," laughed His Royal Highness, "Please lead the way."

"May I offer you my arm, Countess?" asked the young Prince as the old monarch stared at him in astonishment. Where had he learned such social graces, certainly of a more advanced nature than his young life in Montenegro even as a Prince had yet offered him the opportunity for acquiring? Milo began a slight backward "two-step" (so as not to have his back to the monarchy) with Irena on his arm and his mentor beaming approvingly. Nicholas motioned to the two of them to move on ahead of him. He could see it now, that lad one day would be one of Montenegro's best.

The array of food, the likes of which he had never seen before, in amongst the glittering gold and silver serving pieces, ornate candelabras, and sparkling crystal reminded Milo that many hours had passed since he had eaten his last meal at the hotel. Under the tutelage of Irena he went right down the line— some food hot, some cold, Beluga caviar, slices of smoked salmon, sardines, smoked herring, sausages, hot and cold eggs, varieties of cheeses, sauteed mushrooms, ragout of pork, several salads including sliced and marinated cucumber slices in sour cream, beet salad, fine asparagus, and an assortment of breads and crackers.

Milo had never tasted such delicious food in his life. He didn't talk much to the Countess, his mind was on the very enjoyable task at hand. But soon he was comfortably satisfied and he placed his and the Countess's now empty porcelain plates back on the buffet table as he observed other guests doing, and wiped his mouth with the silken napkin. He noticed and thought it curious that, in such a large palace with hundreds of large rooms, everyone stood up to eat while the Czar and Czarina and the Princes and Princesses sat down and did not eat. But everything seemed so strange and unbelievable anyway, even his very being there amidst all this opulence and splendor and being treated for the first time in his life like a grown man. His thoughts were interrupted, for right at that moment twenty or thirty footmen marched into the room through a newly opened door to form a path leading into the next room. The Imperial party rose from their chairs. Conversation ceased. As the Czar and Czarina started toward the newly opened doors, the Emperor turned and motioned to Nicholas and his party to join him.

"Take your places right in back of us," he directed, as the guests moved about to find their proper positions protocol-wise in the processional that would be moving into the next room. This was a serious moment; one must think carefully of titles and official position and not offend anyone of higher rank. Persons of lesser status did not even start to come forward until the procession had moved far enough into the other room to allow adequate space to became available to complete the line.

Upon entering an enormous room with what had to have a hundred crystal chandeliers hanging from the hand painted and gold-leaf ceiling, couples were directed alternately to the right or left and down along a table of seeming unending length. There was a head table and as he followed the Countess, Milo realized that was where they would be sitting. The Czarina sat to the right of the Czar, next to her sat Prince Nicholas of Montenegro, then the Grand Duke Nikolai and Princess Stana, then Prince Milo and Countess Irena. On the other side, next to the Czar sat Grand Duchess Princess Militza and Grand Duke Pyotr, and Grand Duchess Yelena Petrovna, Grand Duke Nikolai Mikhailovich and Grand Duke Dimitri Pavlovich. The top Russian royalty excepted, the men remained standing behind their chairs while the ladies were seated. After the last woman had entered and taken her seat, the men, though unrehearsed, sat down in unison. Almost immediately the first course was served, simultaneously to everyone, by a couple of hundred footmen. Milo smiled to himself; he thought he'd had dinner in the other room, forgetting that Irena had referred to that repast as appetizers. Now he would have to find room for the real dinner.

The ten course meal, served on magnificent gold china, proceeded so smoothly Milo felt as if he were floating on a cloud. The knives, forks and spoons, of solid gold, seemed to offer an extra special flavor as they carried each morsel to the mouth. The sterling silver goblets were filled and then refilled with the finest of wines.

"Are you enjoying our food, Your Highness?" the Countess inquired of Milo.

"Everything is fantastic. I don't know if I'll be able to move after all this."

Irena giggled. She seemed like fun, he thought. With the exception of his sister, Milo had not had much contact with girls so far in his life. However, he was aware of the bird and the bees.

It was the time for toasts, and, at the Czar's lead, everyone stood. The Emperor offered the first one to His Royal Highness, The Prince of Montenegro. It was returned, to the health of His Imperial Majesty. After everyone was reseated, the Czar stood but motioned to everyone to remain seated.

"We take pleasure in welcoming one of our loyal friends of

the court to St. Petersburg. And we have something special for him. This old sword was made in the thirteenth century for a Serb king, Stefan by name, who ruled over a country which at that time included what is now called Montenegro but then called Zeta. That entire land fell into the hands of invading Turks, who absconded with the sword and then lost it. It remained lost for five hundred years. During this time, some courageous Serb people had fled up into the mountains and were able to keep the Turks at bay. This little group were impossible to conquer; they established their own country and called it Montenegro. Recently the sword resurfaced, right here in Russia. It is not Russian; we Russians have no right to it. It belongs to the only Slavic people who never were defeated by the Turks.

The Czar held the sword up so all could see it, a magnificent weapon, encased in gold and studded with diamonds and other precious stones.

"So we have had it refinished, and it is now our honor to proudly give this sword back to the Slavic people of the Balkans, to the person who is the best guardian of Christianity in the Balkans, His Royal Highness, Prince Nicholas of Montenegro. May it protect him and his people against the enemies of virtue and justice and enable them to maintain their unbroken record of historic bravery and valiant achievements."

Clapping, the people rose, as The Czar of Russia presented Prince Nicholas of Montenegro the Sword of Stefan. As Milo watched the two monarchs embrace, pride swelled in his bosom. And a little pressure on his foot under the table sent an unexpected current through his body. He beamed at the fair maiden on his right. This would indeed be a night to remember.

4 | A Russian Odyssey

Count Vorontsov, vice-chancellor under the Empress Elizabeth, assuredly would have been horrified to learn that, some years after his demise, the magnificent palace he called home was transformed into a military academy, albeit, the most prestigious one of in all of Europe, the elite Corps des Pages, whose reputation could best be described by their motto, "We build an elite warrior caste". Count Bartolomeo Rastrelli, the gifted master of Baroque architecture, who also built, at the commission of Catherine II, the Great, the Winter Palace, the Peterhof Palace, and the Smolny Institute for Girls, as well as numerous town palaces for members of the nobility, had been its architect and, undoubtedly, the remodeling job which later enabled it to assume its new role added no enhancements. On the first floor of the school were the administrative and teachers' offices, two small conference rooms, a large dining (mess) hall and a few classrooms. The second floor was given over mostly to classrooms, with a few student quarters; while the third floor was devoted entirely to students' quarters. Milo had a private room on the second floor, while most of the cadets shared an accommodation. Several rooms shared an orderly, a man-servant, who cared for clothing and equipment of the cadets and did certain types of errands for them, thereby freeing their time for study and military practice.

The first few days at the academy brought His Highness up short. Physically in sound shape and highly disciplined, he suddenly found himself lacking in a few very basic abilities. During the issuance of uniforms and equipment he dropped his all over the floor; at drill, when the commander said, "Move to the right in columns of half-sections," he went to the left and found himself wandering off all alone while the rest of his half-section was marching in the opposite direction; and that first night at dinner he had finished only about half of his meal when it was time to get up for the evening's activities. But he quickly learned the techniques of "frantic hurry".

Mornings began with calisthenics before breakfast. After breakfast came parade drill and route march, the goal being fifty miles in ten hours, which is considered even good for a horse. Combat training included combat drill, target practice, battalion drill, and combat exercises including maneuvers using everything from hands and feet to simulated most sophisticated weapons of the times. The activities Milo enjoyed most related to cavalry training, horseback riding, the keeping and training of horses, stable maintenance and equestrian etiquette. Within a few months, many of these exercises moved out of the vicinity of the academy to farther away locations, sometimes fifteen to thirty miles away, and often for durations of several days. In his last two years of study cavalry training become Milo's specialization. He smiled when told that historically the function of cavalry in battle often seemed to be to add a bit of class to what would otherwise appear to be an unseemly brawl.

"So, what's wrong with that?" he laughed.

Lunch was at twelve noon. Academic classes were scheduled in the afternoon: mathematics, chemistry, history and philosophy, military strategy and tactics, logistics, special weaponry, leadership training and terrain reading and training. From three to four there was time for a brief nap and tea, and then two more hours of classes. Dinner was at eight o'clock, which allowed a couple of free hours for individual choices of activities, such as study, cards, billiards, dominoes, skittles or even rest. After dinner came another study-time until lights-out; and although Sunday was a free day, most of that had to be taken for study, too. Sleep became a very precious commodity; every minute of it savored to its fullest.

Right outside St. Petersburg was a great military camp used by the regiments of the Imperial Court for summer maneuvers, Krasnoe Selo. During the summertime, Milo received assignment as a trainee there, a not too unpleasant task among the wealthy and aristocratic young Russian officers. Always reserved; nevertheless, when opportunities arose, he joined wholeheartedly in the conversations and activities of the Russian officers. Due to his height, carriage, and serious demeanor, he was usually taken to be much older than he really was.

From among the best students at the academy a few were also chosen to be Kammerpages and as such were assigned to various members of the Imperial family to serve, when not attending class, upon request, at various court functions. Prince Milo was thrilled to be appointed Kammerpage to his cousin-in-law, Grand Duke Nikolai Nicolaievich. Nikolai was also a General in the Russian army, and during the yet to come World War I served as its Commander-in-Chief until the Czar foolishly took over the job for himself.

In May, 1903, the bicentenary of the founding of St. Petersburg was celebrated; Czar Nicholas II decided its theme should be seventeenth-century Russia. Although he spoke fluent English, French and German, Russian was his language of choice and in his personal life as well as in running his empire, he lived, thought and breathed Russian, in total contrast with one of his predecessors, Peter, the Great, who had been completely mesmerized by Western European culture and had founded the city of St. Petersburg upon the basis of emulating its best and most grand endeavors, and, wherever possible, improving upon them. It was Nicholas' intense nationalism that prompted his choosing the reign of Peter's father, Czar Alexis, as the motif for the Imperial Ball, reversing, at least for one magical night, the influence of the European-minded Peter.

As entertainment for the gala, twenty-four young couples were asked to perform a specially choreographed Russian dance for the event, lessons to be given by Aistov himself, the great ballet master. Quite surprised, Milo was invited to be a part of the group and when he arrived the first day at the dance master's studio, he was even further surprised to see someone he had met before, the Countess Irena.

"Irena, how are you? I did not expect to see you here."

"I'm fine, Your Highness, thank you. Are you disappointed in seeing me?"

"Oh, no. I'm glad to see someone I know," Milo stammered, feeling he was just about to put his foot in his mouth. "I mean I'm really happy to see you." To his surprise, he realized he meant it.

"I'm glad about that."

How very pretty she was, he thought, prettier than any girl he had ever seen; but then he had never paid much attention to any of them before. Her porcelain white skin, with blond curls tumbling down around the neckline ruffle of her cream-colored blouse, rising and falling over the soft, roundness that lay beneath, all made him feel a little differently than he had ever felt before. He didn't understand what it was or why he was feeling that way. But before he could say anything further the dance master called them to attention for the first lesson in preparation for their role at the costume ball.

Concurrently elsewhere, many other guests had begun taking brush-up lessons, or even learning from scratch, some of the old Russian dances that had fallen into disuse in recent years.

"That will be all for today," said Aistov. "We will meet again in exactly one week, same time, right here. In the meantime, I want all of you to practice these steps I have taught you today so that you do them easily and well, without any hesitancy. Even though you are not professional dancers you will want to dance as if you were. These dances are not difficult, but they must be done with precision. You were all carefully selected; you must not let your sponsors down."

"I wonder who thought of me, of all people. I've never danced," exclaimed Milo as he and the Countess were walking out.

"I thought you were very good," Irena replied. "No one would ever guess you had never danced. I don't think you have to worry about a thing. Isn't it fun?" she asked, beaming almost worshipfully up at him.

"Yes, it's not as bad as I thought it would be. I was a bit scared at first."

"You don't have anything to be scared about. Maybe we could do some practicing together. What do you think? With your studies and all, when might you have some spare time?"

"I must practice, so I will have to make time. I think Sunday would be the only day possible for me. Would your parents approve? Where would we do it?"

If you came to our villa, I know everything would be just fine. Oh, here's the coachman; he's picking me up, right over there. Would you like us to drop you off at the Corps des Pages; it's right on our way?"

"Oh, that would be nice. Thank you very much."

The young Prince helped his charming lady friend into the carriage, crawled in after her and the coachman headed toward the academy.

After allowing a few minutes for her friend to adapt himself to his new surroundings, Irena broke the silence, "How are you liking it here in St. Petersburg, and at the Corps des Pages?"

"I like it very much. I'll admit, I've never been so busy in my life. There is a great deal of studying to do, and these extra assignments take up what remains of any spare time. But it's all very interesting and I'm really enjoying every moment."

"I'm glad. It would be horrible if you didn't like it. Oh, we're here already. On Sunday, I suggest you come to our place before tea time. We'll practice first and then have tea, if that's satisfactory with you. I'm sure Mama and Papa will be agreeable to this. Our villa is right off the Nevsky Prospekt at the Catherine Canal; it sort of sits back aways from the street, around a plaza; you can't miss it. Is two o'clock all right with you?"

"That would be perfect", said His Highness, alighting from the carriage. "I am looking forward to it. Thank you for bringing me home." He took her hand and bowed over it, not quite kissing it. He felt its softness, the most delicate thing he could ever remember having touched. "Good-bye".

"Bye". The carriage took off, Irena waving a lace handkerchief and sending back a smile that would have melt a glacier in the East Siberian Sea.

Sunday came around quickly. Milo whistled happily as he donned his elegant Kammerpage uniform, with white gloves and all the accessories, and then called for an izvoshniki to drive him to the Countess Vladmir's residence.

A ball at the Winter Palace was without peer, in any kingdom, anywhere in the world; and no palace in the world was better suited for such lavish revelry as was the Winter Palace. For the upcoming event, the outside of the entire length of the three-blocks-long palace would be flooded with lights; while inside, within its gigantic galleries with their balconies and great columns of marble and jasper, each room the size of a cathedral, huge crystal and gold chandeliers would be ablaze with glimmer of hundred of lights. Masses of flowering trees and huge floral arrangements, counting up into the thousands, would be brought in from however far need be. For this once in every two hundred-year event, occurring, as it was, a month past the closing of the official social season which went from New Year's Eve to the end of Lent, even more elaborate decorations were being created. Because the guests were being commanded to appear in gowns and robes of the seventeenth century, the tailors, dressmakers, milliners, homemakers, wigmakers, of the city found themselves working feverishly into the wee hours of the morning to meet an immovable deadline.

Practicing at the villa of the Countess Irena each Sunday afternoon had enabled her parents to get to know the young Montenegrin Prince and approve of him as a suitable friend for their thirteen-year old daughter. When the evening of the grand ball arrived, they were only too happy to swing by the Corps des Pages with their carriage at seven-thirty to pick him up at for the journey to the Winter Palace. A seemingly endless line of carriages were already drawing up in front of the main entrance when they arrived. Three thousand guests were expected this night: court officials in uniforms of black with gold; generals with masses of war medals blazing on their chests; young officers in full dress uniforms, jackets of brilliant blues, reds and greens, breeches, tight and black; ladies in decolletage of the current fashion enhanced by jewelry of glittering diamonds, sapphires, emeralds, rubies, and pearls, around necks and wrists, on ears and fingers, sewn onto gowns and trains and hanging around varying sizes of waists. Ascending the red-carpeted, wide marble staircase, highlighted by pots of palm trees on the sidelines and massive arrangements of magenta and white flowers woven through trailing greenery framing the huge Louis XIII mirrors, one could sneak that last minute glance to double check that everything was in place.

As Milo walked down the long corridors, he smilingly nodded at a few of the Chevaliers Guards in their silver, breast-plated, white uniforms and eagle-crested helmets. He had performed the function they would be doing this evening several times already that year and actually would have been standing there with them again tonight were he not in the dance troupe. Tonight he was on the other side; he was an invited guest.

Promptly at eight-thirty the Grand Master of Ceremonies appeared, tapped on the floor with his staff, on the top of which was the double-headed eagle of the Czar. Instantly there was quiet throughout the hall as his voice rang out, "Their Imperial Majesties", the Emperor and Empress of Russia". Hugh mahogany doors swung open and in swept Czar Nicholas II and his

Empress Alexandra, he in a red velvet and brocade costume that had belonged to the Czar Alexis, she in a silver brocade gown sewn with diamonds. Dresses rustled as the ladies dropped to a floor curtsy and the men took a deep bow. Tonight would not be a night for the waltz nor polonaise; it was time for the old Russian dances everyone had been practicing, with perhaps an Oriental quadrille and a bit of gypsy music thrown in. To get everyone properly in the mood for the feeling of old Russia, the twenty-four young couples performed for Their Imperial Majesties and three thousand guests, with a grace and precision that bellied their amateur status. Irena and Milo smiled at each other as they took their bows, responding to the overwhelmingly enthusiastic ovation of the audience. A surprising, impromptu request by the Czar for a special dance by a darling of the court, the beautiful Princess Zinaida Yusopova, rounded out the evening's entertainment. Now it was time for the rest of the guests to come onto the dance floor, to dance into the wee hours of the morning.

In adjacent rooms supper was served, while through the double glass of the long windows one could see the city itself, veiled in a bluish haze of silver and pearl. To the east a yellow-pink line became wider as tomorrow came closer. Milo and Irena walked out onto the terrace, the breeze of the late, spring evening and the distant shouts of street vendors arousing their senses.

"What a wonderful evening," exclaimed the Countess. "I think the Czar was quite pleased with our dancing."

"Yes, it has been a wonderful evening. I'm sorry to see it end," Milo replied. "This coming Saturday I'm going with Nikolai, as his Kammerpage, to a flotilla of some decorated yachts that will be parading on the Neva River in honor of the bicentenary, right where Vasilievsky Island splits. It should be fun. Would you care to come along? Would your parents permit you to? Stana would chaperone; I know she wouldn't mind as she is used to chaperoning girls from the Smolny. She remembers you."

-THOM

"I'd love it. I'm sure Mama and Papa would permit it, especially being as we'll be with the Grand Duke and Duchess Nicolaievich."

"I also think Nikolai and Stana would be happy to swing around and pick you up before they get to me, as your home is right on the way to the academy; then we'd head on down to the dock."

"That'd be wonderful. Thank you for inviting me." His Highness and the Countess shared that Saturday cruising the Neva. The following Saturday found them with Princess Militza, and her husband, the Grand Duke Pyotr Nicolaievich, attending the inauguration of the new Troitsky (Trinity) Bridge spanning the Neva. The Emperor and the two Empresses; his mother, the Dowager Empress Marie Feodorovna; and his wife, Empress Alexandra, were in attendance at the event, along with the Mayor of St. Petersburg. For this occasion, Milo served as Kammerpage to Pyotr, assisting him in some small role in the molebin, a short religious ceremony used to invoke a blessing at the opening of an event. The Icon of the Holy Visage, permanently housed in a chapel, originally a log cabin belonging to Peter, the Great, on the Petrovsky Embankment, was brought by boat to the event, as it was to all the ceremonies in which it was used.

Soon the celebrations for the bicentenary came to an end, but Milo decided he did not want this to be an end to his seeing Irena. He wished somehow they could be together alone sometimes; and he expressed this wish to her, much to her pleasure. So they made plans to meet again the following Sunday, just the two of them, in the garden park near the Winter Palace. They dare not go to the Hotel Europa or Astor for tea, and equally out was taking in the Imperial Ballet or the Maryinsky Theatre, because someone who knew her would surely see them. So, as the weeks passed on, they contented themselves with a tryst on a hidden bench in the park or a tete-a-tete at a small restaurant on a side street where they felt they would not be recognized.

It became winter. The nights began early in the afternoon

and lasted until the middle of the following morning. The Neva was frozen over. Cold winds and freezing snow flurries brought out the layered woolen clothing, heavy boots and fur caps, and furs to be worn not only for making an entrance to the fabulous balls but, more importantly, for warmth and protection against the severe elements. The park bench could no longer be used, so the bubbling samovar for a glass of hot tea at their little restaurant brought them inside every Sunday.

This Sunday as they met, Milo walked her past the restaurant and turned at the corner onto an even smaller side street.

"What's wrong?" Irena inquired.

He stopped and turned toward her, tilting her chin up toward his with the edge of his index finger. "I worry about you, about us. Your parents are sure to find out about our meetings one of these days; they will be very angry, and we are both going to be in a lot of trouble."

"Yes, I've thought about that. Maybe we should let a little longer stretch of time elapse before we see each other again."

That was not what had been going through Milo's mind. Then and there, on that tiny side street, he forgot his caution and drew her to him. It was quiet and they were alone; and in his arms she was soft and yielding, his burning kiss not unwelcomed. They held each other tightly, a first for both, afraid that if they let go they would never again have each other. The snow flurries continued swirling around them.

On January 26, 1904, Russia went to war with Japan. Its transport, the "Yenisei", had been sunk by a Japanese mine. One hundred officers and men, together with their commander, were lost. The Russian people did not understand the reason for the war and as the extent of their losses were revealed, public sentiment became deeply troubled. Then on February 6th, two Russian battleships, the "Tsarevich" and the "Retvizan", along with the cruiser, "Pollada", were torpedoed. This last incident pulled the masses together in a united spirit behind the Czar and their Fatherland. Momentarily, there developed an outpouring of love for the Czar such as he had never had before and would never have again; confidence was high that Russian might would triumph over the Japanese. This was Nicholas II's finest moment, but it was only for a moment. Although appreciative, he, correctly, was apprehensive about this sudden, overwhelming public endorsement. He did not understand it, as he had never really understood his people and the basic feelings within the country. A victorious war at that point would have solidified his hold on the nation; but, unfortunately, that was not to happen.

Through the summer of 1904, the war began to unravel and a downward spiral continued through the fall of that year. The following January, Port Arthur, on which Russia had a ninety-nine year lease from China, surrendered to the Japanese. Even though the prospect of a complete Russian defeat was appearing more and more likely, Czar Nicholas, nevertheless, ordered the entire Russian Fleet, then stationed on the Baltic Sea, to travel half way around the world to the Pacific and reestablish itself there. Throughout all of this Nicholas never for a moment stopped to realize that the foreign policy he was following had developed as the result of direct, personal and subtle manipulation on him by his own cousin, German Emperor Wilhelm II. Famed novelist, Leo Tolstoy, thru the good offices of the Grand Duke Pyotr, tried, several times, to warn the Czar that he was heading for a cataclysmic disaster on both the home and foreign fronts, but his warnings fell on deaf ears. The aftermath of all this was that restless workers and students in factories and schools became ripe for influence by the Socialists and Communists who had been biding their time, waiting for over a decade, for the right moment. The mood for war was evaporating; the winds of reorganization, change, and reform were gaining momentum. Strikes became commonplace, everywhere, in the factories, in the schools. Father Georg Gapon, a revolutionary priest with some self-proclaimed noble intentions of bringing together the Czar and the now dissatisfied citizenry, rallied workers for a mass march on the Winter Palace where he said he would hand the Czar personally a petition on behalf of the Russian people.

Milo was back at the Corps des Pages the weekend of January 21, 1905. It was that Saturday that the police learned the march was planned for the following day. By Sunday morning reinforcements for the local troops had been brought in from the outlying areas. Infantry men, backed by Cossacks and Hussars, formed lines at bridges and strategic city corners for the purpose of blocking the marchers rapidly swelling to 120,000 strong. Along with two other cadets, Milo left the academy right after lunch. Together they walked along the Admiralty Prospekt toward the Nevsky. Parents with their toddlers were strolling in the gardens by the Winter Palace, while other children skated on the midwinter ice which had taken over miniature lakes in some of the smaller parks.

It was a bright, sunny day; the mass march had begun about an hour previous, with Father Gapon in his priestly garb at the lead. There were numerous religious banners, flags, crosses, icons, and a large picture of the Czar and one of the Czarina. Then, from behind the Narva Gates, without any warning, a cavalry squadron of the Life Guard Grenadiers rode straight out at the crowd, first breaking ranks, then going to the side, allowing an infantry regiment to come through. The crowd was startled but with hands joined continued ahead singing hymns. A bugle sounded; a shot was heard. Milo and his buddies darted into a courtyard and hid behind the stone wall which was low enough to peer over. What they saw sent them into complete shock; men, women and children falling to the ground, shot by the hundreds, by the Cossack cavalry.

Concurrently, an identical scenario was being played out in many other places throughout the city. On the Nevsky Prospekt at Shlisselburg Trakt, the people were fired upon from the rear, and then after they fell trampled on by the cavalry. On Vasilevsky

Island, six thousand marchers met a detachment of the Finnish Life Guard Regiment who charged the crowd with raised rifles, leaving hundreds of bullet-ridden bodies beside demolished barricades. Within the Palace Square itself, now filled with over 2,000 cavalry and infantry, a detachment of the Preobrazhensky Guards took aim on people, adults and children alike, who were in the garden playing their Sunday games. When the people looked up, they froze; no one could believe what was happening. Milo had led his friends around from the Narva Gates to the Nevsky just in time to see the people near the palace dropping like flies in the snow, people not a part of the march, their bodies spewing forth blood staining the winter landscape a dark crimson. The soldiers fired again and again, wantonly; panic-stricken, the crowd was fleeing in every direction and being pushed back from every direction. There was no more sun.

Then it stopped, almost as suddenly as it had started. There actually had been no confrontation in the real sense of the word; it appeared, in most instances, that soldiers simply fired on unarmed people who did not obey the command, "Halt", and then on others who began running because they saw people falling to the ground. Father Gapon, their leader, vanished, ostensibly after being wounded. The officially acknowledged toll was around a couple hundred dead and several hundred wounded; it probably was double or triple that figure. During all this time, Czar Nicholas wasn't even at the Winter Palace; he was at Tsarskoe Selo, his personal, fabulous dream world, a village symbolizing the most wondrous of cities anyone could possibly imagine, aware not in the slightest of what was transpiring outside of it.

Slushing through the now falling snow, Milo and his friends tried to give assistance, aid, and support to the fallen. Some they could help to their feet, children they carried to enclosures as protection from further cold. Milo wanted to go to Irena but he knew he was needed here to give help and comfort to the many who were hurt. The lights of the Nevsky had not come on; it was black. This was the day that would be known forever in the annals of Russian history as "Bloody Sunday". But it was only the beginning. It ignited what was to be called the Revolution of 1905.

On the afternoon of May 27th, half way around the world, Russia's ill-conceived expansionist movement in Asia came to an end. A barrage of Japanese shells ripped through the Russian fleet in the Strait of Tsushima between Japan and Korea. All eight Russian battleships were lost, as well as seven out of twelve cruisers, and six out of nine destroyers. In forty-five minutes, two-thirds of the Russian fleet was wiped out. Three months later, under the helpful hand of United States President Theodore Roosevelt, a treaty bringing the war to a close was signed at Portsmouth, New Hampshire. On the far side of the globe, the Czar had lost a war, while at home, his country was rushing head-on into a revolution. Leo Tolstoy should have been heeded; now it was too late.

There developed one crisis after another, each more serious than the last. Violence spread to every part of Russia. In mid-October a paralyzing food strike closed schools and hospitals. Newspapers shut down, electric lights went out. The Revolution of 1905 was at hand; its leader was Leon Trotsky. Finally recalling Leo Tolstoy's warning of three years prior, Nicholas summoned his uncle, Grand Duke Nikolai, for some last-minute advice before putting his signature to a document called "The Imperial Manifesto of October 17, 1905". Although this transformed Russia from an absolute monarchy into a semi-constitutional monarchy, it did not go as far as the constitutional monarchy of England. The Czar retained his powers over defense and foreign affairs and the appointment and dismissal of his ministers. The Manifesto did, however, promise freedom of speech, assembly and association; and it officially granted an elected parliament, the Duma (actually established on August 6th, a couple of months previous), promising that no law would go into effect without the Duma's concurrence. Although the document was of landmark proportions, Tolstoy did not think it was strong enough. Conversely, the political establishment viewed it as a sign of weakness. Nobody was willing to help implement the vast changes toward democracy the Czar had put his signature to. Neither the Right nor the Left were happy; the former felt the Czar had betrayed them, the later did not trust him. The country kept right on deteriorating and by the end of that same month, the "Imperial Manifesto" had come and gone.

The spirit of Russia was that of an apocalypse soon to overwhelm the entire country. Every concept, every idea, every thought that been the basis of the old Russian society now was being challenged to its core. There was no sense of past, present or future, no feeling of self or place. The poets, the painters, the sculptors, the writers, the musicians, the dancers, all sensed this so much more than the politicians. Wealthy capitalists and revolutionary intelligentsia found themselves caught up in a melodrama they didn't understand being played out in their everyday lives, one over which they had no control. The psychological atmosphere was that of continuous sorrow, of lives shredded to pieces as avalanche after avalanche of tragedy descended upon an entire population.

Not completely surprising, out of all this there developed a renaissance in spiritual mysticism, a belief in supernatural phenomenon and superstitions. Primitive pagan beliefs that superseded Christianity reasserted themselves; cults arose; people began engaging in seances to communicate with "the other world". The Starets, who were described by Dostoyevsky in his "The Brothers Karamazov" as wandering pilgrims who "absorb your soul and will into their soul and will, as you give into them willingly in utter submission," arose to prominence. Milo's cousins, the Grand Duchesses, Militza and Stana, typical of extrovert, fashionable ladies of high society everywhere, bored with the routines of excessive wealth and unmeaningful religion but always at the forefront of the newest and latest trends, enthusiastically embraced this Oriental brand of mysticism that had become so popular overnight in the society mansions of the capital. Militza's magnificent palace at Sergeyevsky on the Angliskaya Nabereznaya (the English Quay) became a central meeting place for Grand Dukes and Princes and their consorts to gather behind drawn velvet draperies for their own special seances.

One evening Milo was invited to a dinner party at Militza's. Totally unaware of his cousins' penchant for the superstitious and hypnotic, luckily he neglected to ask if he could bring Irena that night. The guests were quite international, just as her mansion reflected an interest in traditions other than Russian, rugs from Persia, paintings from France, tapestries from Austria-Hungary, statuary from Italy, in rooms of paneled mahogany, parqueted floors and marble colonnades and balustrades.

French was spoken that night, and Milo was carrying on a lively conversation with Militza's sister, Stana, perhaps the more beautiful of the two, when the room suddenly became quiet. An eerie feeling crept over him, as he realized there was someone unusual in back of him. He planned to turn sideways to see who it was, when Stana spoke out.

"Gregori, you have arrived. We could not do anything without you. But first, I want to introduce you to my cousin, Prince Milo. Milo, this is Father Gregori Rasputin, our honored guest from the Kronstadt Monastery, one of the Starets, a mystical prophet and divine healer."

Gregori Efimovich Rasputin, known simply as Rasputin, presented himself as a humble penitent who had received a command to do God's work. Long, greasy hair growing into a tangled beard falling down over a plain black caftan which didn't quite cover his peasant's dirty boots, he seemed to view his ugly and dirty appearance as a validation of his spiritual persona. Nonetheless, he carried with him credentials from the highest clergymen. But it was the eyes that had it . . . piercing, deep blue-gray, exuding an exhausting depth of hypnotic power, mesmerizing whomever was the focus of his momentary attention.

Milo's mouth almost fell open, but not quite. With a nod, he acknowledged the introduction. Why was this man here; what did he want of his cousins? There was no way Milo nor anyone else would possibly suspect that what Rasputin was working toward was a personal introduction to the Czar and Czarina of Russia.

The two Montenegrin Princess sisters whispered briefly, and then the room was darkened. Candles were snuffed, and everyone was directed to a seating in a circle, men and women alternating. To Milo's utter surprise, Militza and Stana took seats on either side of Rasputin, each taking one of his hands for the evening seance that was about to begin. Milo sat through it all patiently, as another man, the "medium", mumbled a bunch of indistinct words while the flames from the few candles left burning illuminated the surrounding faces.

The evening concluded with tea from ornate silver samovars, washing down elegant, little pastries, accompanied by haunting melodies pouring forth from the violins of three gypsy entertainers. When Milo said his good-byes for the evening he assumed he would never see this man again. He was wrong.

It was only a couple of weeks later when Stana invited him to her house at Znamensky and the same thing happened again. The lamps were not lit; in their place candles burned in front of large icons, with guests standing in a half circle, as if in a trance, occupied with thoughts of "spiritualism". Rasputin was there, Stana giving him her complete and adoring attention, trying to anticipate his every need. Her husband, Grand Duke Nikolai, was absent this evening. Milo looked around him, thinking what a disgustingly spoiled and ill-adjusted group of people these were. It was at this moment he felt his first disillusionment with Mother Russia.

It began in 1718 as a surprise gift from Empress Catherine I to her husband, Peter, the Great, this handsome stone country house with gardens and arbores and linden trees. This was Tsarskoe Selo, "the Tzar's Village", fifteen miles south of St. Petersburg, standing on 1680 acres of lush landscaped parks and magnificent gardens. In 1741 when their daughter, Elizabeth, came to the throne, she thought less in terms of a stone country house but more in terms of a "Versailles", and employed Bartolomeo Rastrelli to build such a place for her. This he did, on a stupendous scale, an ornate blue and white structure of over two hundred rooms. Gold leaf on oil adorned everything, ornaments, pillars, balustrades; word circulated that even the roof was made of solid gold. Elizabeth named it the Catherine Palace in honor of her mother, Catherine I. In the middle was an artificial lake, big enough for small sailboats, surrounded by monuments, arches, bridges, a Chinese pagoda and theatre as part of a little Chinese village, kiosks and a pink Turkish bath. It was considered the world of the "earthly gods", a legendary place, a pampered community to which only a very few people had right of entry.

A second palace, a simpler one only fifteen hundred feet away, built later by Catherine II, the Great, and named the Alexander Palace after her grandson, became the favorite of Nicholas II and Alexandra. It was here they spent much of their time, a graceful two-story classical building of just over one hundred rooms. It was to this "home" that Milo was invited for a few days at the end of October, 1905. Magnificent parks and exquisite gardens surrounded the two palaces, all encircled by high iron fences patrolled by bearded Cossacks on horseback, marvelously handsome in their black fur capes, red tunics, boots and sabers. From 1905 to 1913, the year of the celebration of the tercentenary of the Romanov dynasty, Tsarskoe Selo was where the Imperial family maintained their permanent residence, not the Winter Palace in St. Petersburg where they were actually in attendance only a couple of times during all those years.

In startling contrast to the lavish splendor of the rest of the palace, Milo remembered for the rest of his life the small study

71

with its plain, comfortable leather chairs, in which Nicholas II greeted him upon his arrival, the room in which the Emperor spent most of his time while at Tsarskoe Selo. In this simple, intimate setting, Milo had his first private conversation with the Czar of all the Russias. A basically quite, shy man, the monarch seemed genuinely happy to be able to talk in an informal manner to someone who wasn't trying to manipulate him or get something out of him and their conversation continued unabated until dinner was announced at eight o'clock sharp.

Although these were strictly family affairs, the Empress always dressed for dinner in evening gown and jewels. Their four daughters, the Grand Duchesses Olga, Tatiana, Marie and Anastasia (she had the same name as Milo's cousin, who usually used her "nickname", Stana, so as to avoid confusion) joined the dinner table. Their one son, the Czarevich Alexi, remained in his room, bedridden with the frightening disease, hemophilia, a disease afflicting males but carried through the female lineage of a family, in this case through Queen Victoria. At that moment, he was hemorrhaging internally and had muscle spasms in his legs; two nurses continuously ministered to his needs. Dinner was a quiet affair, conversations were in English as Alexandra preferred it. Afterwards everyone sojourned to the drawing room, where Nicholas normally would either read aloud to his family or everyone would look at or arrange photographs in family albums, photography being the favorite hobby of the Imperial family. Tonight it was different; they did not do any of this. Czarevich Alexi had suffered a set-back earlier in the day when he inadvertently fell and within seconds was helpless. The physicians had been by his bedside ever since; tomorrow the Imperial family was expecting the arrival of a specialist to see if he could help the Crown Prince.

This was the first time Milo had spent a few nights as the house guest in the home of another family, not to mention such an august family. Aside from the grave situation of the heir-apparent, the overall feeling of Imperial Majesty faded from Milo's consciousness, and for awhile it seemed almost like being home. Behind the pomp and grandeur of their positions, at Tzarskoe Selo the Czar and his family were just like any other family, with the same sorrows and tragedies to face, but in their case, with the additional overwhelming burden of empire.

The next day, November 1st, to Milo's surprise, the Princesses Militza and Stana arrived with their husbands, the Grand Dukes Pyotr and Nikolai. He had no idea they would be there and wondered why they had arrived separately from him, when through the door walked—Rasputin. So this was the specialist they were expecting! The Grand Duchess Stana had visited the Czarina just a few days prior, to remind her of the great healing powers and wonders ascribed to the Starets, and to Rasputin in particular. Alexandra, who had always had a religious zeal and mystical streak, admitted that she had longed to meet the monk and have him visit Alexi. Stana had responded to that desire in haste and that afternoon the little Czarevich's pain, fever and muscle spasms vanished.

Rasputin rose overnight to become the sensation of the inner court circle. As a result of his seeming mystical powers to help control or even appear to cure the incurable hemophilia that kept the Czar's son, Alexi, on a roller coaster of sickness, he soon became the spiritual advisor and finally the political advisor to the Czar and Czarina. In observing this new arrival to the court of Russia, Milo could only wonder what Nikita back in Montenegro would think of it, and of his two daughters so under the spell of clairvoyants and faith healers. On the day Rasputin's influence at the Imperial Court commenced, Milo's desire to return home commenced. A few years later, in 1911, after Milo had returned home, and after years of scandalous behavior on the part of Rasputin, the Grand Duchesses Militza and Stana swore off their former protege. By that time, when they tried to tell the Czarina they now believed Rasputin to be a fake, she would not listen to them, even though they were the ones who had introduced her to Rasputin. From that day on, the friendship between Empress and the two Montenegrin princesses cooled.

During this same year, opening and playing to a full house at the Volksoper in Vienna in 1905 was the beautiful operetta, "The Merry Widow, music and lyrics by Austrian-Hungarian composer, Franz Lehar. Inspired by the country of Montenegro, Lehar wrote a precious fairy tale story about a fictitious beautiful but poor country called Marshovia, or Pontevedrian, and a wealthy, young widow named Sonia, whom the country's ambassadors wanted their Prince Danilo, to marry, so as to keep her money in the country. When she takes a trip to Paris, she puts them all in a tizzy; and so they send Prince Danilo to Paris, also, to woo her back home. This is fine with him; he loves Maxim's and the all the girls in the can-can! Now even if you haven't seen the operetta you can probably guess what happens. In the 1930s the real Crown Prince Danilo brought a successful law suit against an American film company, because of Erich von Stroheim's portrayal of him in that film. That was, perhaps, a poor casting choice for the role of Danilo; but a more enchanting operetta has never graced the stage nor the silver screen.

The Czar enjoyed young Milo's company; and in April, 1906, he and Alexandra invited Milo to spend a few days in the Crimea with them, and to join them for the trip down on the Imperial train, that string of luxurious blue and gold salon cars with the gold, double-eagle crest on either side of each car, all pulled by a shiny black locomotive. The luxury inside was equal to that of the Imperial palaces. The dining car easily took a table for twenty, with crystal chandeliers, velvet drapes, polished floors, panelling of the finest mahogany and upholstery in soft shades of mauve and gray, those being the Empresses's favorite decorating colors. A special lounge car was set aside for the ladies, complete with deep-piled rugs, satin-covered chairs and sofas with matching pillows, and all the necessary accoutrements for the toilette.

The trip was slow, two nights and a day, accompanied by the underlying fear that the train might be blown up at any time by revolutionaries. It wasn't. They weren't yet ready.

It was Easter time; and the seaside hills of the Crimea were filled with groves of cypress trees, orchards, vineyards, shrubs and wildflowers. Roses, magnificent in size and color, draped over buildings and walls, and in the background rugged mountain peaks rose up from the turquoise waters below. Livadia Palace, a wooden structure, which, five years later, in 1911, would be foolishly replaced by something more elaborate, was a favorite of Nicholas and Alexandra. High posts mounted by the familiar golden eagles marked the Imperial land, and to each side beautiful villas of the aristocracy nestled between the cliffs and the sea. One of these belonged to Princess Militza, and her husband, Grand Duke Pyotr. It was called Dulber. Within thick walls and built like a fortress, years later it would offer the Grand Dukes and Duchesses a safe haven from the Bolsheviks until eventual evacuation by the British would save their lives. The hand of fate, however, would not be so kind to the Czar, Czarina and their children.

Milo stayed with his cousins at Dulber during his few days on the Black Sea. He spent most of his days outdoors, swimming, riding horseback, playing tennis, sailing. Easter Sunday reminded him of his Easters in Montenegro: the sumptuous eating, which broke the severe Lenten fast, began right after the Eastern Orthodox church services and continued on for at least two days and a night. There were also the beautifully decorated Easter eggs; but these were the real ones, not to be broken in some silly, childish game. Some of the eggs were simple but beautifully painted egg shells from which the eggs had been drawn out through tiny pinholes. Others were magnificent, gem-decorated wonders wrought by the master jeweler, Peter Carl Faberge. Each year it was Nicholas's practice to order two Faberge eggs, one for his wife and one for his mother. The masterpieces Faberge created for Nicholas II and his father, Alexander III,

HOM

totaling fifty-six in all, became more and more complex each year. The piece-de-resistance was one he designed in 1900, the Great Siberian Railway Easter Egg. Faberge's works have survived as symbols of a vanished era of lavishness and splendor, but also of an era of craftsmanship and beauty, the likes of which have not been seen since, and may never again.

The glory of Easter and the outpouring of joyous and happy emotions almost made Milo forgot the things he had seen and felt which bothered him, but not quite. Grand Duchess Olga, the Emperor's sister, gave a ball one night; Milo chose not to attend. From his room at Dulber he could see Livadia and the guests strolling in the gardens when they were not dancing to look at the hugh springtime moon casting its silver light across the shining waters of the Black Sea. He knew things were not like this everywhere; what he didn't know was that they would not be like this much longer here ever again.

In 1906 the Duma, or parliament of Russia, was inaugurated at the Winter Palace in St. Petersburg. For the first time, representatives of the people, all the people, assembled in one room. On one side of the hall were the ministers and advisers, the military and civil functionaries, and the courtiers, while on the other side were the newly chosen representatives of the people, of the landowners, the lawyers, the merchants, the noblemen and the peasants. Functioning as Kammerpage to Duke Nikolai, Milo had the opportunity to witness this memorable event, an historic moment that never left its mark because too many of the participants did not bother to put forth the effort needed to make it a success. Even the Empress was against it, declaring that the people were not well enough educated for it, and that an autocracy was what Russia should remain. So, no matter what anybody did, the empire just continued to crumble.

1907 began Milo's two years of specialization at the Corps des Pages in advanced cavalry training. This took him to the different regiments, cuirassier, uhlan, hussar and dragoon, the latter being the largest. Arms study included saber, rifle with bayonet, and lance. Unique to Russia among cavalries were the Cossacks of the Imperial Guards. Milo had arrived in St. Petersburg an accomplished horseman; and never, not even once, did any Russian student surpass his equestrian skills.

The pressure of school had lightened considerably, and so the young Prince had more leisure time. The first electric trams, adding to the former horse-drawn ones, were put into operation that year, as were buses, so more and better transportation was available to the masses. It was easier for students and workers to get around and Milo, now seventeen, was seeing Irena quite a bit more frequently, but always, of course, with chaperones. On November 25th, the prima ballerina, Matilda Kchessinska, former sweetheart of Nicholas II prior to his marriage to Alexandra, had to withdraw at the last moment from performing in "Pavillon d'Armide" and it was announced that taking her place that night, dancing opposite Vaslav Nijinsky, would be Anna Pavlova. Irena had expressed such admiration for Pavlova that Milo felt certain it would delight her to attend the performance. He obtained three tickets, of course, one for the chaperone, but on the morning of the performance, Irena's mother did not feel well. Papa said he would take her place, but on the way to the theatre he "remembered something he had to do" and let the young couple go on alone.

The Prince took his lovely Countess to the Astor Hotel for a before-the-theatre dinner, a post-theatre dinner being out of the question, much too late for such a young, royal couple, and chaperoneless!

It was a night of enchantment for them both, ballet at the Maryinsky, seating 2,000 of Russia's aristocracy in its sumptuous blue and gold interior tiers of seats and boxes, the Imperial box, centered and girded by two big golden eagles. The audience was enveloped in luxury and opulence. Everywhere were smiling, happy, beautiful faces, adorned with jewels, furs and gowns of satin and brocade. At the end of the second act, a little boy dancer by the name of George Balanchine was called out to

77

MY FATHER, THE PRINCE

take a special bow. Years later that name would become an almost household word in the field of dance choreography. Milo
and Irena were quite tickled at seeing this; he was so much
younger than they, it made them feel positively mature. Also in
the audience that night were Their Imperial Majesties and after
the final curtain, the youngster was taken to the Imperial box to
be presented to them. They gave him a chocolate-filled silver
box. Years later George Balanchine was quoted as saying the
Czarina's beauty compared favorably with that of movie star-
Monaco Princess Grace Kelly.

During these years the department store of Yeliseev Brothers, the Fortnum and Mason of St. Petersburg, was built at 56
Nevsky Prospekt. Decorated with bronzes and large panels of
stained glass, it was the quintessential, grand-scale, elegant deli-
catessen store. In the late spring of 1908, on a Saturday or Sunday
afternoon, Milo and Irena would often meet there, perhaps for a
concert in the hall on the second floor, then afterwards to the
foyer to choose among the delicacies lining its buffet tables. On
the third floor was a small room for smaller concerts or chamber
music. An intimate afternoon was often spent here, talking, holding hands, sharing their fears and aspirations, dreams and desires.

One weekend day a year was visiting day at the Smolny
Institute for Girls. His Highness, dressed in his winter uniform
of black tunic with gold collar, cuffs and buttons and black trou-
sers with a thin red line down the side of each leg, white gloves
in hand, joined the Count and Countess Konstantin Vladmir,
Irena's father and mother, to attend the special event. Built within
the confines of the Smolny Convent, its founder, Catherine, the
Great, had been determined to provide serious education for
qualified daughters of European nobility. Girls entered the institute at age six and left at eighteen. Irena was in her last year.

This was a special afternoon, with the girls providing varying types of entertainment for their guests. In the main hall they
all had an opportunity to participate in dancing for their parents
and friends; then outside on the lawn, after donning wide-brimmed

frilled muslin hats, practiced players squared off in some fine tennis matches under huge shade trees. During tea a trio of harpists, including Irena, entertained the assemblage. All of the leading royalty and nobility who had any relatives at the Smolny were in attendance; the event was a highlight of every year.

In their slowly-drawn carriage heading for home at the close of the day, they passed the newly completed Church of the Resurrection, known as Church of the Savior on the Blood, because it was built on the spot where Alexander II fell victim to an assassination. Erected on the quay of the Catherine Canal by Alexander III, right in the heart of St. Petersburg, it remains an assertive statement of the Slavophilism the Czar Alexis promoted prior to his son, Peter the Great's, pro-European influence. With over 7,000 square meters of mosaic covering the interior and exterior, its onion domes, similar in overall appearance to St. Basil's in Moscow but more richly and elaborately ornamented with thousands of semi-precious stones, its uncompromising Russian style bolstered the innate character of the people living in this beautiful city that had come to reflect the culture of another place and had forgotten its own. The Slavophilism of the architecture of the Church of the Resurrection reflected the continuing efforts of Nicholas II to regain more cultural expression of an uncontaminated Russian heritage.

After the four of them alighted from the carriage to take a long and close look at the magnificent structure that had been under construction since 1883, they went inside.

"This is the real Russia, isn't it?" asked Milo to anyone who wanted to answer.

The Count replied, "Yes, and we seem to be on the road to losing it. I hope, my son, you can keep the real Montenegro at home."

"I hope so, too," replied a startled Milo, not certain exactly what he meant but feeling a premonition, like of a storm brewing that you can faintly smell before you can feel it or see it. "I have learned so much since my arrival, things not in the books

79

HOM

nor taught in the classrooms, things I never dreamed existed. Yours is a country almost too gigantic to grasp in thought."

"That is its problem."

"We are so small in Montenegro. We should not have that problem."

"No, but you can have others."

"Yes, yes, I guess you're right." Milo looked down at the blood-stained cobblestones as they departed the church.

"Milo, Their Imperial Majesties have invited us to be guests on their yacht, the "Standart", for a cruise on the Baltic. Would you like to join us?" the Count asked, glancing, as he spoke, at his daughter who was about to burst with joy. "For him, the school will excuse you, I'm sure. I think we'd be gone about a week or so."

"Oh, that would be wonderful. On the Emperor's yacht. Wow.! Oh, I'm sorry, I didn't mean to be so——"

"Don't worry," said the Count laughingly, "I know how you feel."

Ten days later, the Imperial family and their guests boarded the ketch, the Alexandra, at the Peterhof Palace, for the trip to Kronshtadt, where the Imperial yacht, "Standart", was moored. Besides the Czar and Czarina, the party included their four daughters, the Grand Duchesses Olga, Tatiana, Marie and Anastasia; their son, the Czarevich Alexi; the Emperor's sister, also named Grand Duchess Olga; the Empress's sister, Grand Duchess Elizabeth; Milo's cousins and their husbands, Grand Duke Nikolai and Grand Duchess Stana, Grand Duke Pyotr and Grand Duchess Militza; the Grand Dukes Nikolai and Sergi Mikhailovich; Grand Duke Dimitri Pavlovich, the Czar's nephew; Grand Duchess Yelena Petrovna; the Countess Irena Vladmir and her parents, the Count and Countess Konstantin Vladmir; Prime Minister Peter Stolypin; and Prince Milo. Several other guests were on board, also.

These were wonderful times on the blue sea, with warm, sunny days and cold, starry nights, probably one of the few times the royal family and their closest friends were totally relaxed, with all tensions left behind. Milo and Irena spent most of the time together, enjoying the stops at sandy beaches for swimming in the surf, walking along the shoreline and picnicking in little, out-of-the-way coves. This day, lying back on the shaded grass, listening to the sound of the soft waves and feeling the gentle breezes through the spruce trees, the two were quiet, just holding hands. Off shore, the "Standart" was moored, some of the guests sunning themselves on deck, a couple of the brave ones diving into the ocean, others enjoying a game of cards under an umbrella.

"Milo, when you go back to Montenegro, will you remember Russia? Do you think you would ever come back? Would you like to live here, or is that out of the question?"

Milo heaved a sigh. "I love it here in Russia. I am having a wonderful time, and I love being with you; but I don't know what is going to happen up ahead. When I go back I will immediately join the Montenegrin army as an officer in the cavalry. That is where my life is. Do you think you would ever come to Montenegro?"

"I would love to. But Mama and Papa, I don't think, would be too keen about that idea. It's sort of a small country, you know; and they think Russia is the very best place to be. It's very nice for us here, don't you think?"

"Oh, yes, you have so much more of everything than we have. Ours is a simple, mountainous country; and your parents wouldn't like it. Then there is Prince George of Greece, you know. Your parents haven't given up on their idea for you to marry him! So, all in all, things are a bit difficult for us, aren't they?"

"Oh, don't talk like that! You know I don't like Prince George; I don't think he's at all interesting, and he certainly isn't very handsome."

Holding her hand tightly in his Milo said somberly, "I love you, Irena. I don't want to hurt you or cause you any grief".

"I love you, too, Milo. I fear that we shall soon part and never see each other again; when your school is over you will go back to Montenegro and forget all about me."

"I'll never forget about you. After I am back and in the army and settled, you can come over."

"Maybe," was the very soft reply.

"I think we should go back to the ship. I'm sure they're wondering about us already." Milo helped Irena to her feet and picked up the remains of the picnic things. At the ship the crew was making plans to move on. The passengers were in their staterooms resting or beginning to dress for dinner as they came on board and headed for their cabins. Milo tilted her chin up as he stood in front of her cabin.

"I love you," he whispered, and then went down the hall to his stateroom.

Milo spent his most of the spring of 1909 concentrating on his final studies and practices; he wanted to return home an outstanding soldier, an excellent marksman, and the best cavalryman in Montenegro. Prince George of Greece had been invited by Irena's parents to visit St. Petersburg and much to her displeasure she was kept busy. Milo knew he was not ready to take a wife, but when he did he knew he should take a full-blooded Montenegrin lady as had done Prince Nicholas before him. Russia had always been good to little Montenegro but he was not Russian, he was Montenegrin, a part of their royal family, and his entire life would be devoted to the service of his country.

One afternoon toward the end of his sojourn in Russia, His Highness was to meet the Grand Dukes Nikolai and Pyotr Nicolaievich at the Imperial Yacht Club on Morskaya Street for dinner. With a membership of under one hundred and fifty, this club was the ultimate in snob appeal. Its elegant premises, outstanding cuisine, and congenial atmosphere where friendships were formed, careers made or broken, was in a class by itself. Milo had left Nikolai and Pyotr only a short while ago at the Znamenskaya Square where he had attended the dedication of the Prince Troubetskoy sculpted monument to Alexander III, serving as the Kammerpage to them both. Six years in the works, the unveiling of the statue finally took place on May 23rd to a mixed reception. A rather stolid, ungraceful figure on horseback, it went against typical heroic images, reminding one of the figures of those ancient Russian warriors, the bogatyri, again reflecting Nicholas II's preference for the culture and feelings of old Russia.

Milo would be going home at the end of the week. As he sat in the grandiose yet somewhat gloomy reception hall of the Imperial Yacht Club, awaiting his cousins for a final dinner, just the three of them, he observed and listened to the men of importance and position in the Russian empire as they arrived to meet friends for dinner. Talk was about an approaching revolution, agrarian disorders, the burning of factories. Here came Count Alexi Alexandrovich Bobrinsky, and there went the Grand Dukes Nikolai and Sergei Mikhailovich with Saavva T. Morozov, a wealthy industrialist from Moscow, who played the game on both sides by often backing Bolshevik and other revolutionary causes for his own pecuniary advantage. Circumstances do make strange bedfellows or some such thought crossed Milo's mind as he watched the passing parade.

It was none too soon, his going home. Milo was homesick for Montenegro.

HOM

5 | Montenegro Betrayed

Prince Milo couldn't wait to report to the Army Barracks at Cetinje, headquarters of the standing army of Montenegro. He had left home seven years ago a boy, eager to prepare himself for this moment, and had returned a man, ready to place his life in the service of his country. The commanding officer responded to his salute and signed him up personally.

The permanent army of the little principality of Montenegro consisted of but one battalion and a small force of artillery. Every year, however, an additional 4,000 men passed through its ranks, each receiving an intensive four-month training, at the end of which time was issued a modern magazine rifle and cartridges for which he was held accountable. Every man from age sixteen to sixty was a soldier in the army. Throughout the country, once a week, on Sunday, there was drill and inspection of weapons for all able-bodied men. Those selected to be officers were sent for an additional four months training to the Officers Training Corps of Russia, Italy or France. For most of them, this was their first trip out of the country, and how they did enjoy the extra-curricular activities this opportunity brought! Though small when compared to the armies of the larger countries, with some financial help from the Czar, Montenegro's was considered among the best. Prince Nicholas had reorganized it and it had proven its metal on numerous occasions.

The soldier's uniform was basically a slight variation of the national costume: for the enlisted men a sleeveless vest of heavy gold with silk embroidery over a long white or pale blue coat called a gunj, over blue pants, with the ever-seen "kapa" on the head; for the officers, a more elaborate version of the national costume, a short red jacket with embroidery matching the vest, its sleeves hanging hussar fashion over the back or over the sleeves of the shirt under the undervest. The insignia on the rim of the "kapa" indicated the rank of the soldier. Only His Royal Highness had a round insignia; an officer upon whom the honor of Senator had been bestowed by the monarch had a double eagle and lion made of brass; lower officers had different combinations of crossed swords; while the simplest insignia was a star made of lead, worn by the corporal. Officers also sometimes wore the more typical officer's uniform with a brimmed cap. Within a short period of time Milo was awarded the honor of Senator and with it came its insignia for his "kapa". One would think a cavalry would be of little use in such a mountainous country as Montenegro, even though there were some stretches of flat land, but it had evolved as one of the more important branches of its military. Many soldiers had horses and rode well. Milo, his future as a ranking officer in the cavalry of the Montenegrin army easily and quickly secured, rose rapidly to become Assistant Chief of Staff of the Lovcen Division, and later, toward the end of World War I, was the Acting Chief of Staff of the Kotor Division.

Between the years of 1906 and 1914, fierce economic and industrial rivalry arose amongst a number of European countries, and as a result there developed patterns of countries forming alliances, mutual trade pacts or military agreements they would be called today. The architect for the first alliance was Chancellor von Bismarck, when he persuaded the Austrian-Hungarian Empire to become Germany's ally. Russia soon joined that alliance but then she fell out and Italy took her place, so there was founded what came to be known as the Triple Alliance: Germany, Austria and Italy, later called the Central Powers. Over on the other side, Russia, France and Great Britain formed the

Triple Entente, so called because it resulted from combining the Dual Alliance of Russia and France on one hand with the Entente Cordiale of France and Great Britain on the other, the combination later to be referred to as the Allies.

Yugoslavia had not yet come into existence as a country: Montenegro was a separate country, as was Serbia. Croatia and Slovenia were southern provinces of Austria; and Bosnia-Herzegovina, as per the Congress of Berlin in 1878, had been placed under the occupation and administration of Austria even though actual possession was still vested in the Ottoman Empire.

In 1906, in a fiasco dubbed "The Pig War", Austria-Hungary refused to import her ally Serbia's most important export, hogs, because Austria believed them to be diseased. In retaliation, the Serbs dropped their alliance with the Austrians in favor of France and Russia, both of which offered them the hog markets they needed. Thus did Serbia begin her alliance with France, an alliance that would stand her well during and after the yet-to-come World War I and one that would portend the tragedy that was to befall Montenegro.

In 1908, ostensibly to forestall rumored plans by Serbia to move into Bosnia-Herzegovina, Austria completed her control of these two provinces by taking official possession. Serbia was furious, as was in fact much of Western Europe; and so it was at this point that conspiratorial plots against Austria began fomenting. King Peter of Serbia (widower of Princess Zorka of Montenegro) severed all ties with Vienna. Time would prove that Austria's move, occurring as it did in the same year as the Diamond Jubilee celebration of Emperor Franz-Josef's sixty-year reign, was highly unwise politically and poorly timed psychologically. It is said that World War I began in Sarajevo, Bosnia, on June 28, 1914, with "the shot that was heard around the world". It really began six years earlier in that same country, when Austria took one step too far to tilt the balance of power in southern Europe.

During this time, throughout Central and Southern Europe, varying species of nationalism were arising, from the subliminal to the more open and pronounced, curling their tendrils over and around each other. In 1910, combining some nationalistic pride with a personal dose of ego, Prince Nicholas changed Montenegro from a princedom into a kingdom. Instead of being Their Royal Highnesses, he became His Majesty, King Nicholas, and his wife became Her Majesty, Queen Milena.

Just across the Adriatic, Italy was seething with jealousy over France's colonial acquisitions in Algeria, Tunisia and Morocco. To counterbalance the French in North Africa, Italy decided she wanted Libya. To get it, in September of 1911 she declared war on Turkey. By the following year, even after recently having had her military reorganized by the Germans, and having closed the Straits of Dardanelles, Turkey found her forces outnumbered and outclassed by the Italians. Through the Treaty of Ouchy, she not only had to cede Libya to Italy but she had to give up Rhodes and the Dodecanese Islands as well. Two days later, not even given time to lick her wounds, Turkey was invaded from another source!

Macedonia, at varying times over the centuries dominated by Bulgaria, Turkey and Serbia, was, in 1912, a part of the Turkish empire, when reports of atrocities committed by the Turks on the Macedonians reached Serbia. Her hopes for expansion had been given a set-back in Bosnia-Hercegovina, but these new reports about Macedonia provided her with a much-desired pretext for instigating a combined Balkan retaliatory attack against Turkey. Serbia, Bulgaria, and Greece already had formed The Balkan Alliance for the express purpose of eliminating Turkish power in the Balkans, the result of which, of course, would increase their own territorial boundaries. Now with Turkey's weakened position after having lost its war with Italy, the Balkan Alliance decided this would be an ideal time to eliminate Turkish power in the Balkans by embarking upon a conquest of Macedonia, for the "noble purpose" of freeing it from Turkey.

The recent German-trained Turkish forces numbered about 240,000 in the invasion area. Bulgarian forces numbered 180,000 men, Serb 80,000, and Greek 50,000, each having about the same number of well-trained reserves in back. At the invitation of Serbia, Montenegro, unwisely, was only too happy to help her Slav sister; Montenegro's militia strength of 30,000 was highly capable in the area of guerrilla operations. This, the first of two Balkan wars, and Milo's first battle, commenced October 17, 1912, with all four of the allies moving simultaneously into Turkish provinces. By the end of the year Turkey was defeated, but not without a little post-mortem. Right after the Bulgar-Serb siege of Constantinople, while the armistice was being declared, Greece and Montenegro on their own faced up to some behind-the-scenes Turkish forces still fighting at Yannina and Scutari. The Serbs had already departed the area. On April 22, 1913, under the command of Prince Milo, the final Turkish forces in Scutari fell to the Montenegrins.

Then came the dividing of the victors' spoils. In her constant pursuit for an outlet to the sea, Serbia had been promised the area which is now Albania, as well as half of Macedonia, with Bulgaria receiving the other half. But Austria, ever fearful, and perhaps rightly so, of any increase in Serbian power, was able to garner the support of Great Britain and Germany for the purpose of making Albania an independent nation. On May 30, 1913, an uneasy Treaty of London, signed in Bucharest, Bulgaria, was imposed upon the participants of the First Balkan War by the Entente powers. Montenegro was asked and agreed to abandon Scutari to the newly formed country of Albania, in return for only an insignificant frontier extension. However, when it came to the division of Macedonia, Bulgaria on one hand and Serbia and Greece on the other could not come to an agreement; and by the first of July, the Second Balkan War commenced between these countries. After a couple of weeks the Rumanians, and even the vanquished Turks, intervened on the side of

Serbia and Greece against Bulgaria, the net result being that Bulgaria lost all she had gained during the First Balkan War.

Montenegro, who had not instigated either of the wars, and who had entered the first out of loyalty to her neighbor and "friend", Serbia, received very little as a result of her efforts to help her Slavic sister. Serbia, on the other hand, almost doubled in size as a result of these two wars. Her ambitions for expansion were now thoroughly aroused and her hatred for Austria, and consequently also Bosnia-Herzegovina as a part of Austria, grew daily almost like an uncontrollable cancer. Germany, who had recently reorganized Turkey's military only to have it lose two wars in succession, was feeling rather humiliated by it all but went right back to Turkey and reorganized them—again, at the same time, of course, strengthening the bonds that tie.

Among the three great powers that maintained influence and power in the Balkans, Austria-Hungary, Turkey and Russia, only Russia refrained from getting involved in the Balkan Wars. The Grand Duke Nikolai, now Commander-in-Chief of the Russian Army, under the strong urging of his wife, Stana, the King of Montenegro's daughter, wanted to send troops to support Montenegro in the First Balkan War and Serbia the second time around. However, upon the advice of Rasputin, the Czar not only decided to remain neutral but he removed Grand Duke Nikolai as Commander-in-Chief of the Russian Army and appointed himself to that position. This was a childish and foolish reaction; Nikolai was viewed by many Russian people as a more qualified Romanov than Nicholas II and was even considered by some a possible Czar replacement. Rasputin, on the other hand, whether saint or satan, because of his life's experiences, understood the world so much better than did the Czar. The wily old monk did not like war, and he also saw clearly the intensity of the internal cataclysm barreling down upon Russia, and upon the Czar. His advice to the Czar, undoubtedly, was the correct one under the circumstances. Had it not been followed, World

My FATHER, THE PRINCE

War I probably would have started a year earlier, without "the shot that was heard around the world". In either event, however, the final outcome for Imperial Russia, unfortunately, would have been the same.

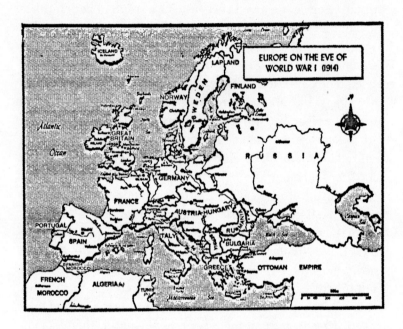

On June 28, 1914, in Sarajevo, capital of Bosnia-Hercegovina, the era of comfort, confidence and gentlemanly, ladylike behavior in Europe came to a screeching halt. While on a State visit to Sarajevo, walking along the main boulevard with his morganatic wife, Her Grace, Sophie, Princess of Hohenberg, Archduke Franz-Ferdinand, the heir to the Austrian-Hungarian throne, and his wife, were assassinated. A young Bosnian-Serb student, Gavrilo Princip, and two associates, were accused of the murder; but it was alleged that the crime had been committed on orders from higher ups, possibly from "The Black Hand", the terrorist organization made up of high-ranking Serbian officers that possibly had masterminded the murder of King Alexander and Queen Draga of Serbia some eleven years earlier. There was even some talk that the assassination idea might have been the brain-child of Serbia's king himself, Peter Karageorgevich, or that of his son, Prince Alexander, who, just one month prior, on June 14th, had assumed the position of Acting Regent due to his father's advancing years.

Having had attended as a youth with King Nicholas the wedding ceremony of the now-assassinated couple, Milo felt a personal sadness at their deaths, and being very much aware of Serbia's deep-seated hatred for Austria, he couldn't help but wonder what ill this event forebode. One month later he found out. On July 28th, Austria declared war on Serbia and the very next day she bombed Belgrade.

Without reservation or even waiting to see what any other nations would do, and in the face of Austria offering her large monetary and territorial compensations for having given up Scutari and North Albania after the Balkan Wars to keep out of the current fray, when Serbian King Peter's son, Regent Prince Alexander (also the late Princess Zorka's son) arrived in Montenegro to ask his grandfather, King Nicholas of Montenegro, for his support, King Nicholas immediately promised unlimited military assistance to Serbia! There were those close to Nicholas who advised him to stay out of the war, that Montenegro was too small to get involved, but true to his strong feelings of Serbian ethnic loyalty, that advice fell on deaf ears. That very day he wired Prime Minister Pashich of Serbia as follows: "Serbia may rely on the unconditional support of Montenegro at this moment on which the fate of the Serbian Nation so much depends, as well as on every other occasion."

Out of a population of less than half a million, the entire army of Montenegro, 53,000 men, was immediately mobilized. King Nicholas sent ultimatums to all the enemies of her neighbor (imagine little Montenegro sending ultimatums to such powerful countries as Germany, Austria-Hungary and Bulgaria!). Serbia, Greece and Montenegro signed an alliance for both defensive and offensive purposes, which agreement the Greeks later repudiated while Montenegro pledged her entire country's resources to the defense of Serbia. Montenegro's small force then invaded giant Austria.

This time, on July 30th, Russia did mobilize her army in defense of her Slavic neighbor, Serbia, causing Germany to retaliate by declaring war on Russia the very next day. On the 4th, Great Britain declared war upon Germany, who already had started trying to knock out France, Belgium and Luxembourg before they could mobilize their forces. World War I was underway.

By September, Montenegro had penetrated through Herzegovina and half of Bosnia as to as far north as Sarajevo, all then part of Austria, while the invading Austrians had been forced out of Serbia. Ostensibly to guarantee a unity of command on the Balkan front, Serbia asked the Montenegrin government to place all its troops under Serbian command, that of General Boris Yankovitch and General Pierre (Petar) Pechitch. As a result, the Montenegrin General Staff was now composed of Serbian officers! King Nicholas, seventy-five years of age, remained Commander-in-Chief of the Montenegrin army and continued to take an active part in the war. For a year, though lacking in numbers and now getting short of ammunition and equipment, Montenegro fought tooth and nail along side of and for Serbia. At this point the world was astonished; these two Balkan countries were holding their own against insurmountable odds. Then came the crucial moments. Bulgaria joined hands with Austria. Greece withdrew from the tri-lateral defense and offense treaty she had with Serbia and Montenegro; she may have learned a lesson or two about Serbia during the Balkan Wars that apparently little Montenegro had not. Rumania prudently chose to remain neutral a bit longer, while on October 29th, Turkey joined the Central Powers; now it was Austria-Hungary, Germany, Bulgaria, and Turkey—making it four. Serbia seemed doomed.

In 1915, an Austrian force of 25,000 attacked 700 men at

the Montenegrin fort at Kuk; even with such overwhelming numbers, it took them three days and two nights to take it. Talk about fighting against overwhelming odds, yet the Montenegrins were later accused by the Serbians of having retreated too soon!

During all this time, the United States was keeping to the sidelines, even though by now she was the chief supplier of munitions and other war materials to France, Britain and Russia. After the Cunard luxury liner, the "Lusitania", was torpedoed off the Irish coast on May 7th by a German U-20 without any warning, 1,256 lives lost, 124 of them Americans, feelings for involvement began rising rapidly on the western side of the Atlantic. On May 23rd, after much postponing and procrastinating, Italy declared war on Austria; then, three months later, on August 24th, Rumania finally decided to join the battle on the Allies' side, too. Greece still vacillated, as did the United States.

In July, 1915, under severe pressure from Premier Pashich of Serbia coupled with threats of "breaking off relations", and in his advancing years desirous of maintaining harmony with his fellow Serb, King Nicholas made the fatal mistake of relinquishing the ultimate control of the Montenegrin army, the supreme command, to the Serbians!

When the Central Powers renewed their attack on Serbia in September of 1915, she was attacked on all sides. French and British forces moved to assist her, but the Allied intervention arriving at the Greek port of Salonika was too little and too late. They were also in the undesirable position of being on neutral territory, with the Greek army posturing and threatening their rear.

By October of 1915, the Serbian army was completely demoralized; everywhere soldiers were laying down their arms and withdrawing before 60,000 advancing Austrians. A Montenegrin force of fifteen thousand self-sacrificing soldiers covered their withdrawal, thus saving the Serbian army as well as hordes of civilian Serbian refugees, and making possible their retreat

THOM

through snow-covered mountains into Montenegro and Albania, and in some cases, on to Salonika, Greece.

On November 17th, Serbian Regent, Prince Alexander traveled to Cetinje to personally thank his grandfather, King Nicholas, for saving his and his Father's lives in October, as well as those of his troops. On the 9th of December, Prime Minister Pashich of Serbia, the very one who had forced King Nicholas out of the supreme command of his own forces, repeated the same mission to express his gratitude. On the surface it seemed to be a time for gratitude to Montenegro, but already the ground work for treason by its own allies against the tiny kingdom was in the making.

That act of treason commenced on Christmas Day, 1915, when 43,000 Austrians with 640 guns and two naval divisions, attacked Mount Lovcen, where Prince Milo commanded 5,000 Montenegrin soldiers, with but eighteen guns and 1,500 shells amongst them. Serbian officers stormed in and commandeered most of these supplies for their own troops, leaving the Montenegrins with practically no arms at all. Still, the Montenegrins fought for three more days until every last piece of ammunition was gone. Montenegro had intentionally been "hung out to dry". Then, to continue this deception, on the morning of December 29th, General Pechitch, the Serbian Chief of the Montenegrin General Staff, on behalf of the Serbian Prime Minister Pashich, who, only a few weeks before had thanked King Nicholas for saving the lives of their King and Prince and many of their troops, went to King Nicholas and ordered him to ask the Austrians for a truce. Realizing finally he was being betrayed by the country he had gone to help defend itself, Nicholas refused; but, old and weary, he was finally worn down and agreed to ask for an armistice under the condition that they, the Serbs, publicly take responsibility for the action. This they agreed to do, but never did.

When the flag of truce was raised atop the fortress at Mount

Lovcen, the Montenegrin soldiers wept. Three of the army brigades immediately disbanded. There was nothing left for Milo to do. In defiance of the Serbian General's orders to remain on site, along with his best friend, Major Marko Popovich, and a group of fellow warriors, he fled into the mountains and headed toward the front at Salonika, Greece, where they hoped to join in the fighting there. The Serbian High Command, its orders ignored, was furious and decided to destroy this little group of rebels, their own allies! But to cover itself it first sought out concurrence for its plans from the French High Command. Successful in this endeavor, the Montenegrin brigade was captured and shipped to Corsica, where they were to be shot. Prince Milo stood in line facing the firing squad. The shot in his chest which pierced a corner of his heart but left him alive would have called for a second round and certain death but for naval gunfire close by momentarily distracting the firing squad, thereby enabling Major Popovich and a couple of his men to drag Milo into hiding, and in the ensuing confusion and under cover of the late day's deepening shadows, to eventual escape. The remaining soldiers, not enemies but allies of their captors, were interned as prisoners of war and not released until 1919 when they were set free at the same time as the enemy German prisoners-of-war were freed.

It was only after the war was long over, and too late to be of any help, that Pravda, the Belgrade newspaper controlled by the Serbian Ministry of Foreign Affairs, revealed how General Pierre Pechitch, one of the Serbian commanders of the Montenegrin Army, had openly boasted about how he intentionally placed the Montenegrin army in the position that capitulation to the Austrians would be inevitable and the annihilation of Montenegro thereby assured. Asking Austria for peace made King Nicholas and Montenegro appear perfidious in the eyes of the world, exactly as Serbia intended; and as a result, much of the monarch's prestige, at home and abroad, was destroyed. The Montenegrin people and its army were demoralized and confused by their leader's actions, while the Serbs had accomplished what they wanted. They never assumed responsibility for the action they had laid on King Nicholas, but instead, went on the offensive and openly accused Montenegro of being traitorous to the Allied cause by asking for the truce, when it was they who first left the Montenegrin army defenseless and then conceived of the idea of Montenegro asking for a truce, forcing the deed on King Nicholas.

A few months later, in April, 1916, in Fribourg, Switzerland, a full two years before the final armistice ending the war was signed, Prince Sixte of Bourbon disclosed another conspiracy against Montenegro, that secret negotiations for peace had been entered into between England and France on one side and Austria-Hungary on the other. The conditions for peace, as suggested by the French Government, were, that to appease both Austria and Serbia, the two warring factions that had started the war, Montenegro be divided between them, the former to get the Mount Lovcen area and the latter the rest of the country! Was this was ever spoken of as treason, the allies planning to sell out one of their own? Yet Montenegro had been accused by Serbia of being traitorous to the Allied cause when Nicholas, based upon a Serbian General's coercion, broke down and followed that Serbian General's orders and asked Austria for a truce.

In January of 1916, surviving Serbian forces which had arrived in Salonika were transferred by Italian and French ships to the island of Corfu where they were reconstituted by the Allies and in July transferred back to the Salonika front, 118,000 strong. Serbian General Pechitch made a point of not allowing either King Nicholas nor any Montenegrin soldiers to even put in an appearance at Salonika. He wasn't about to run the risk of Montenegrin soldiers being permitted to re-equip themselves with ammunition, food or clothing. At this time in Montenegro there were about 50,000 Montenegrin soldiers left with seventy out-of-date cannons, pitted against 138,000 Austrians with over 1,000 guns and two naval divisions standing off the coast.

Serbia used the Austrian occupation of Montenegro as an excuse to move some of her own troops into Montenegro, ostensibly to "stand by" her poor little neighbor, although throughout all of 1916 both Montenegro and Serbia were occupied by Austrian troops. Successfully hiding her treacherous intentions against the nation which so heroically had been fighting by her side all the time, Serbia, at the end of the war, plain and simple, planned to incorporate tiny Montenegro into the kingdom of Serbia. Not yet having had her lust for conquest satiated, she would gain her territorial expansion by occupying Montenegro, and at the same time, achieve her goal of an outlet to the sea.

His Imperial Majesty, Emperor Franz-Josef, the frail Commander-in-Chief of the Austrian-Hungarian Army, never saw the end of this war, the war he had begun because of the murder of his nephew and heir by a fanatic young Serb; he passed away in November, 1916. And a man whom he had always greatly admired and whose country he had not wanted to fight, His Majesty, King Nicholas, along with members of his immediate and extended family, including Prince Milo, and high Montenegrin government officials, were forced into exile from Montenegro to seek refuge elsewhere. For the first time in her history, Montenegro had fallen, and for the first time in five hundred years she was occupied by an enemy, in this case two enemies: Austria, whom she had foolishly gone to fight, and Serbia, her "friend" and ally, but now her "hidden enemy", whom she had foolishly gone to fight for! The royal family accepted the proffered "hospitality" of another supposed ally, France. Unaware of the secret Swiss negotiations where France had not only been a major participant but the proposer of the plan to give most of Montenegro to Serbia, when offered exile in France the royal family gratefully accepted and walked right into the lion's den. They settled in Neuilly, France, on the outskirts of Paris. Due to occupation by the Central Powers, both King Peter of Serbia and King Albert of Belgium had abandoned their capitals a

97

considerable time before King Nicholas was forced out of his. When the war was over, these two were allowed to return to their thrones; Nicholas was never allowed to return to his.

Far away in St. Petersburg, an old friend of Montenegro, Russia, was being torn apart. While in the midst of fighting a world war, she was simultaneously internally engulfed by a massive revolution. Nonetheless, she took time to attend a meeting of some of the Allies' Foreign Ministers on March 24, 1915 to state her opposition to the deceitful plan being presented by the treasonous Foreign Minister of Italy, Baron Sidney Sonnino, (his country's own Queen a Montenegrin princess!) to cede Montenegro to Serbia! Serbia's tendrils had reached in every direction across Europe in an effort to position itself for its eventual conquest of Montenegro; but even in the midst of the horrendous upheavals facing Russia, the Imperial Empire took a stand on behalf of its special little Balkan friend.

Prince Felix Feliksovich Yusupov, the richest man in Russia, and his beautiful wife, Irina, who was the Czar's niece, enjoyed entertaining lavishly at their palace on the Moika Embankment. On December 29, 1916, they threw one of their elegant dinner parties, the guest list including Montenegrin Princess Militza and her husband, Grand Duke Pyotr; her sister, Princess Stana and her husband, Grand Duke Nikolai; Grand Duke Dimitri Pavlovich, the Czar's nephew and . . . the religious fanatic, Rasputin, still a close confident of the Czar, through, by now, quite disliked by and distanced from the Grand Dukes and Duchesses. There, that night, in the cellars of his own palace, Prince Yusupov murdered, in a cold-blooded, drawn-out, predetermined manner, the monk, Gregori Rasputin, while, upstairs, unaware of what was happening beneath them, the guests drank and chatted gaily as they waited for their host and a couple of the other guests to return. Rasputin had predicted that he might die by violent means, and that if he did, Russia would, also. Both predictions came true. Although it is known that the Czar's nephew, Dimitri, was the second of the three assassins, it is not known if Montenegrin Princess Stana's husband, the Grand Duke Nikolai, the removed Commander-in-Chief of the Russian Army, was upstairs or in the cellars at Rasputin's moment of truth.

Russia had mobilized 15,000,000 men for war in Europe; but due to indolence and scandals in the top echelons of the government, which had resulted in massive corruption, plundering, and greed, she was totally unable to hold up her end of the fight on the Eastern front. Second and third wave soldiers, who were sent into battle without rifles and with inadequate shoes, clothing and blankets, quickly froze to death or died of gangrene. This army of betrayed men became bitter, now full of nothing but hatred and contempt for the Czardom. Mutinies broke out. Food riots, which quickly spread throughout the country, developed into revolutionary insurrections. There was no longer any confidence in anything; the people were sick of Czars, wars and "Great Powers". Russia was impotent to do anything but watch as a danse macabre did it leaps and pirouettes and pas de chat, from palace to military academy, from villa to cathedral, out to the towns and small villages in the countryside, and on across Siberia, as all the while other figures crept stealthily closer to the throne.

Sunday, February 26th, 1917 was the day of the headless revolution. All of Petrograd (St. Petersburg) was in the streets. It was not possible to deter the citizenry from their plan of action, the overthrow of a now hated regime. Czar Nicholas II and Czarina Alexandra, as usual, were not in St. Petersburg, but were at their beautiful fantasy village, Tsarskoe Selo. They were not yet aware, however, that they were now its prisoners.

Under the leadership of a rather eloquent and moderating man named Alexander Kerensky, a new republican-type of government timidly came to power. Unfortunately it survived but a few months until, on November 17, 1917, under the leadership of Nicolay Lenin, power was seized by the Soviet Government of Bolshevik Socialists, and the moderating Kerensky Government was ousted. It was during this period in August that Czar Nicholas II and his family were transferred from Tsarskoe Selo to the governor's house at Tobolsk, an old Siberian town. Disorder and massacre prevailed everywhere throughout the country. Soldiers shot their officers, peasants butchered their landowners, members of the nobility were liquidated by their servants.

One day in April of the next year the Imperial prisoners were moved for the second and last time, to Ekaterinburg, the former home of the Ipatiev family, now dubbed "The House of Special Designations (Purpose)". There, on July 17, 1918, Czar Nicholas II and Czarina Alexandra and their five children were herded into the cellar of the house and shot. That night, witnesses alleged, the bodies were loaded onto a truck and taken to a mine where they were chopped up, burned, drenched with acid and thrown down an abandoned mine shaft. The official government statement was that the family died during an "evacuation". No bodies were ever recovered until seventy-five years later in 1998 the decomposed bones of most of the victims, including those of the Czar and Czarina were brought back for a proper burial in Moscow.

The Romanovs were no more, but in death they became even larger than in life.

Russia already had "passed out of the war", and now, for all practical purposes as she had been known she "passed out of the world". The light of Montenegro's friend had been extinguished, right about the time her own light was being snuffed out.

Finally, on April 6, 1917, almost three years after the war had started, after the unarmed French steamer "Sussex" was sunk with several more American lives lost, and plots by the

Germans to embroil Mexico in a war against the United States were uncovered, upon receiving Congressional approval, President Woodrow Wilson declared war on Germany. The Yanks were finally coming, better late than never. The revolution in Russia had ended the month before; already withdrawn from the war, she had concluded her own peace treaty. The Austrians were all over Serbia and Montenegro, and by October they had captured 200,000 Italians and had demoralized that country.

All during this time numerous peace proposals were being made by many parties; some later returned to haunt their authors, others still should. The most famous of all the proposals was President Wilson's program of Fourteen Points which he incorporated in an address to Congress on January 8, 1918. For Montenegro the important Point was:

Point Eleven: Restoration of Rumania, Serbia and Montenegro, with access to the sea for Serbia.

On July 4, 1918, in Neuilly, France, King Nicholas received the following telegram from President Woodrow Wilson:

"I trust that Your Majesty and the noble, heroic Montenegrin People will not be cast down but will have confidence in the United States to see that in the final victory the integrity and rights of Montenegro will be secured and recognized."

What joy and relief this telegram must have brought old King Nicholas.

That month a massive offensive was launched against the Germans by the British, French and American troops; and by the end of September such shattering blows had been dealt the Central Powers that they were weakened beyond any hope of return. The war had been going on for three years and the enormous strain was showing clearly in the faces of the entire European population. Services and conditions to which private citizens were normally accustomed showed acute deterioration, and in many cases had been discontinued. The usual honesty

101

and security of every-day life and the disciplined politeness of peacetime behavior had been replaced by the roughness and frequent brutality of military law and order.

Little by little each of the Central Powers left the war, the next to last being Austria, who, on November 3rd, 1918, signed an armistice and withdrew her troops from the Balkans, including from Montenegro. Germany was left alone in the fight against the Allies; but stricken and defeated, on the 11th, she, too, signed her papers for an armistice. The war was over, but it had accomplished nothing in the way of abating militarism or nationalism.

Prince Milo returned to Montenegro, along with some of the members of the Montenegrin Government, the advance guard for the immediate royal family, only to find the Serbian army occupying the country! They explained they were there until King Nicholas and the rest of the government returned and all of the Montenegrin soldiers were back, many of the latter having been interned in Austria, not to mention those that had been held on Corsica. It was not long, however, before Milo began to wonder why King Nicholas wasn't returning, and why the French Government sent a French General, Franchet d'Esperey, along with French troops, to take possession of all the strategic places in the country.

On November 26, 1918, with King Nicholas being held against his will in France, and the majority of the Montenegrin soldiers still not back in the country, authorities from the Serbian government, with the French serving as the "Allies' representative" to give the deed an appearance of official sanction, pulled together at Podgorica an assemblage of two hundred men, some of them Montenegrins too old to have fought in the war, others not Montenegrins at all but Serbians. Under the awning of Serbian bayonets, this group of two hundred hand-picked men were informed that they had just become the Montenegrin National

Parliament, without any semblance of having been duly elected by the Montenegrin people in a free, constitutional election.

All the while, the real government of Montenegro was being detained in France against its will by Premier Georges Clemenceau and future Premier Raymond Poincare and not permitted to leave. It had been only two days previous that the French government, by means of a letter from Clemenceau through the medium of the Allied troops stationed in Montenegro, guaranteed in the name of all of the Great Powers, "to respect the liberty of the Montenegrin People and of its Constitution". It further decreed "that all orders were to be given in the name of the King of Montenegro."

An election was held by the newly established "National Parliament" to determine whether Montenegro should become a part of Serbia or remain an independent country. Under threats of Serbian imprisonment and torture, of course, the vote was favorable for Montenegro to become a part of Serbia. Free for five hundred years, now during the forcible detention of her king and government in France, Montenegro had her liberty stolen from her by a couple hundred hand-selected, mostly unquali-fied men, held hostage at the point of Serbian bayonet, while a large percentage of the country's male population still had not yet returned home from the war. Prince Milo and the soldiers who were already home could not believe their ears when they heard the staggering news . . . Montenegro had been placed under Serbian yoke. So much for French Premier Clemenceau's guarantees. The betrayal of Montenegro was a "fait accompli", its extinction achieved.

The country was now filled with Serbians, well-armed and holding all supplies under their control. Montenegro had sacri-ficed half of her army and one-third of her population during the war on behalf of the Serbians, and now Montenegrin women and children were starving and could not obtain food nor medicine without first acknowledging Serbia as their country. Already re-duced to involuntary servitude through hunger, torture, pillage,

rape, and murder, a veritable reign of terror was unleashed against
the civilian population, now victimized further by unbelievable
cruelty: five thousand houses burned to ashes, less than five
percent of homes escaping fire or pillage; wooden nails driven
under the nails of Montenegrin women to force them to reveal
the whereabouts of their husbands, brothers and/or fathers; cats
tied up under the skirts of helpless Montenegrin women, their
skirts sewn up and the animals inside beaten until they bit and
tore the skin of the helpless women. These acts were later confirmed by articles published in the 1922 and 1923 Belgrade
daily newspapers, Le Balkan and the Tribuna. In 1924, in a
speech to the now Yugoslavian Parliament in Belgrade, a member of its Croatian delegation and a Montenegrin delegate told
the assembly of their witnessing some of the atrocities unleashed
against the Montenegrins: men's eyes being gored out, children
being thrown out of windows onto bayonets (Serbians seemed to
like to kill people by throwing them out of windows—they had
done that with their own former King Alexander and Queen
Draga so would they be any more gracious to the Montenegrins?),
women's and children's arms being broken while others were
massacred by cannon fire.

It was not the first time Montenegro had been assailed by a
powerful foe. For five hundred years, the brave warriors of the
Black Mountain had maintained their freedom at the point of
the sword; often there had been an enemy envious of their tiny
mountain home and threatening to take it away from them. In
the past, the enemy usually had been the Turk but Montenegro
had always been a match for the armies of Islam. Among Balkan
countries, Montenegro had the proud record of being the only
country never occupied by the Mohammedan invader. But this
time it was different; this time the enemy was an ally, its brother
Serb. Montenegro was at a complete disadvantage; having given
them free access to their land, Serbia now controlled all supplies of food, medicine, clothing, weapons, everything. With the
French supervising the occupation and cooperating with the

Montenegro Betrayed

Serbians by supplying money and arms to the Serbs and forceably detaining King Nicholas and his Government officials in France, there was only one course left. The few Montenegrin men available, three thousand strong, under the leadership of Prince Milo, decided to strike one last blow for freedom against this horror and injustice which was being inflicted upon them.

Holding secret meetings, something difficult to do with Serbs everywhere, suspicious of every move the Montenegrins made, Milo and his soldiers finalized their plan of action. The army, or what remnants of it that were back from foreign soil, were to attack the Serbs while a small band of soldiers under one of Montenegro's former parliamentary leaders was to take Cetinje. But before even the initial stages of the plan could be put into action, five of the Montenegrin leaders were captured by the Serbs, while one just managed to avoid capture and fled to Albania. Disaster was staring them straight in the face but they were determined not to submit without a fight. On Christmas Eve, 1918, at eight o'clock in the morning, the three thousand warriors, armed with only rifles, led by Prince Milo and Major Popovich, descended from their hillside hiding places around Cetinje and attacked the well-armed Serbian force of fifty thousand. For three days the battle raged. On December 28th, the Commandant of the Allies' troops(French) in Dalmatia and Montenegro, General Venel, issued the following order:

"The fighting must cease at once and the insurgents return home; there should immediately be re-established telegraph and telephone connection and transportation around and between Bocche di Cattaro and Cetinje, both to become effective at the same time, for the purpose of distribution of food, etc. If this order should fail to be followed, I will take proper measure with the intervention of the army (French)."

To that, Prince Milo answered, "You have not been invited here to command us and tell us what to do in our own house. Go to France and there command whom you have. Leave us alone in peace, that we may, as always, without your intervention, put

105

our country in order; for your power, remember, will not last very long."

The fighting continued for three more weeks; but Serbian troops, under French protection, drove the insurgent Montenegrins from their own capital, Cetinje, and got control of all of the connections that led from Mount Lovcen, near Cetinje, to Bocche di Cattaro (Bay of Kotor). From their remote location, the feeble complaints of the Montenegrins were never allowed to reach the outside world. General Venel "invited" them to lay down their arms; but they chose instead to retreat, fighting as they went.

It was at this point that Prince Milo went to Njegusi, his birthplace, not far from Cetinje, to seek the advice of an American commandant who had just arrived with a detachment of American soldiers. If the American understood what was happening, surely he would do something. The Americans were for freedom and liberty—they said so. Together, the two military leaders met in a tiny room with no electric light, where they could speak privately; the manager of the hotel brought in three or four candles for modest illumination. It was there that Prince Milo requested the advice of the American commandant, explaining that all of Montenegro was occupied by Franco-Serbian forces, who were only interested in maintaining their grip on the pitifully outnumbered Montenegrin insurgents who simply wanted to regain their country's independence; and that, while King Nicholas was held in forced exile in France, millions of French francs were being spent on bribing the Montenegrin population in order to insure Montenegro's being a part of Serbia, thereby becoming the vassal of France in the Balkans.

The American took a long time to respond. Then he said, "I regret not being in a position to help you; for I, too, as well as my detachment, are under the command of the French General."

Prince Milo than asked him to tell him truthfully whether or not there was any hope that the Allies would fulfill the promises they gave to his country.

The American did not like having to answer this question; but after a pause, he said, "Take this into consideration, what I now tell you. Do not believe the promises, no matter from whom they came, for those promises are false. Furthermore, I advise that you, together with your colleagues, seek safety at once, wherever you know it to be, out of the country. If, but even if only until tomorrow, you should remain in the country, it is most likely that you will pay with your lives."

After a two-hour conversation, Prince Milo shook hands with the American commadant and expressed his gratitude for the frank discussion. He then took his leave.

That night, high up in the mountains, the Serbs were determined not to let this small band of Montenegrins retire in peace. There were several skirmishes and a couple of narrow escapes from death. Prince Milo and his compatriots were completely surrounded. Due to the darkness and the mountainous terrain, the Serbs, tired and certain they had the Montenegrins beaten, decided to wait until dawn to take them hostage. Early that January morning in 1919, while the Serbs were settled down to a hefty breakfast, Milo and his small band of Montenegrin patriots broke right through their ranks. By the time the Serbs had recovered from shock and were ready to fire at them, the Montenegrin soldiers were well away, quickly and skillfully making their way through the cragged mountains down to the sea. A number of them fell to the enemy; but those who were fortunate enough to make it to the Adriatic found a several Italian warships lying in waiting off the Dalmatian coast, waiting to help any Montenegrin who needed it. The Queen of Italy, Elena, a Montenegrin princess, would do her best to see that they were not let down; Milo had always been her favorite cousin.

As the ship on which the weary band of brave Montenegrins had taken refuge plowed through the wind-whipped waves toward Bari, Italy, and Milo watched the beloved mountains of Crna Gora disappear into the background, the words of Alfred Lord Tennyson seemed, as if by magic, to float in through the air:

"They rose to where their sov'ran eagle sails,
They kept their faith, their freedom, on the height,
Chaste, frugal, savage, armed by day and night
Against the Turk; whose inroad nowhere scales
Their headlong passes, but his footstep fails,
And red with blood the Crescent reels from flight
Before their dauntless hundreds in prone flight
By thousands down the crags and through the vales.
O smallest among peoples! rough rock-throne
Of Freedom! warriors beating back the swarm
Of Turkish Islam for five hundred years,
Great Crna Gora! never since thine own
Black ridges drew the cloud and broke the storm
Has breathed a race of mightier mountaineers."

On June 28, 1919, the fifth anniversary of the murder of Archduke Franz-Ferdinand, in the beautiful Hall of Mirrors at Versailles the Treaty of Versailles was signed. It applied primarily to Germany, the last country to surrender, as separate pacts had already been concluded to settle matters relating to the other countries. Most of President Wilson's Fourteen Points had long since fallen by the wayside.

Point Eleven, providing for the restoration of Rumania, Serbia and Montenegro was modified in such a way as allowed Rumania to double her territory and Montenegro to be swallowed up, not by a victorious enemy but by an ally in victory, Serbia! The brave little country was no more. Montenegro had a double betrayal.

Seventy-one years later, in September of 1990, upon the occasion of Iraq's overnight invasion and occupation of its neighboring country, little Kuwait, President of the United States George Bush and Soviet President Mikhail Gorbachev jointly issued a statement from Helsinki, Finland, declaring, "No peaceful international order is possible if larger states can devour their smaller neighbors." Six months later the United Nations armed forces led by the United States routed Iraqi soldiers right out of Kuwait. But it had happened during the end of the First World War to little Montenegro and not one of the powerful Allies on whose side she fought came to her rescue.

Lest it be thought that not even a single person among the Allies came forward to champion the cause of Montenegro, it should be noted that the following statements were made by the attributed personages:

On March 11, 1920, during Parliamentary Debates in the British House of Lords, Viscount Gladstone observed that every Power present at the Peace Conference of 1919 had agreed that Belgium and Montenegro should be restored to their post-war status, and stated, "Nevertheless, if Montenegro, instead of joining the Allies, had joined the Central Powers and fought against us, she could not have been treated worse than she has been during the last year and a half."

On November 29, 1920, Lord Sydenham endeavored to re-awaken the House of Lords to a realization of Montenegro's anguish and England's responsibilities. "By what right had King Nicholas been deposed and the Sovereign State of Montenegro blotted out from the map?" he asked. He went on to recapitulate a definite promise of His Majesty's Government, as given by Mr. Asquith, the Prime Minister, on January 20, 1916, "Belgium, Serbia and Montenegro will be restored. England will constantly carry on the war until the restoration of Serbia and Montenegro."

Mr. David Lloyd George, Prime Minister the following year, stated on September 7th, "Serbia, Montenegro and Rumania: the day of their restoration will also be the day of deliverance of the world".

To this remark Lord Sydenham drew the following conclusion: "If these words have any meaning, My Lords, surely the honor of this country is pledged up to the hilt to restore to Montenegro her independence." He went on to recall that the Under Secretary for Foreign Affairs had declared that "all the good offices of His Majesty's Government, as far as they can be effective—and we are not without weight in the Councils of Europe—are at the disposal of the Montenegrins."

But on December 15, 1920, when Lord Lamington, on behalf of Lord Sydenham, followed up on the matter and questioned the Government about the progress on behalf of Montenegro, he received the astonishing reply that it would be "premature to express any decision or final opinion" as to the state of Montenegro.

The most extraordinary crime in the history of small, independent nations had been masterfully perpetrated as the little country of Montenegro was successfully eliminated from the face of the earth by its friends and allies.

Helena Smith in the dress and hat she wore the day she met
the Prince in 1927 in London.

Prince Milo in London, 1930.

Milena, age 6, sitting at the fountain in front of Doheny Library at the University of Southern California in her small size "kapa," where her mother, Helena, received her Ph. D., April 1934.

Prince Milo in Dublin, 1941.

Prince Milo by his Daimler in Dublin, 1945.

The Prince holding his baby daughter, Milena,
6 1/2 months old, 1929.

The Prince's wife, Helena, and daughter, Milena,
in 1932 in Los Angeles.

6 | A Prince Without a Country

Weary and bedraggled, boots filled with mud and covered with debris, a small band of expatriated warriors wearily limped up to the Rome's Palazzo del Quirinale. Located on a high spur of the Roman hill that bore its name, the palace was an architectural marvel, a masterpiece. Begun in the 16th century by Pope Gregory XIII on the site of the former villa of the Cardinal Ippolito d'Este, it took three centuries to complete and became a monument to the genius of the Italian artisans of those centuries.

Queen Elena of Italy, not even trying to hold back the tears streaming down her face, burst through the Palace's Maderno entryway to greet her war-weary cousin with outstretched arms, extending her hands further in welcome to his comrades.

"Milo, my dear, I so feared you would not make it out alive. We knew the French were there to back up the Serbs as they finished their take-over, all the while keeping Father and Mother hostage on the Cote d'Azur and telling the rest of the world that they had sold out their country and looted Montenegro of millions. I know from first-hand witnesses they've had no freedom of movement whatsoever and are just making do with the barest of necessities. This whole situation has been unbelievable. But, I mustn't talk to you about this now. You are totally exhausted. Let me take you and your men to your quarters."

As she walked through the door she looked back to see that the men hadn't moved; they were just standing there, looking down at their mud-ridden boots. Laughing, she motioned them to come on, reassuring them it was all right to walk on the carpet. A plush maroon, bordered on all sides in a gold serpentine pattern, it led straight through the stately reception hall to the wide stairway rising to the floors above. The guest wing was on the third floor, and here the Montenegrin soldiers were assigned suites of a elegance never seen by any of them before. Further on down the hall, Prince Milo and Major Popovich were shown to the most magnificent of all, quite on a par with those Milo had seen at the Imperial palaces in Russia.

Elena, too, had spent her childhood and adolescence in at the Court of St. Petersburg, receiving her education at the Smolny Institute for Women. As a result of those years in Russia, often spending many summer vacations with Czar Alexander II's family (he was her godfather), she acquired the poise and demeanor that was the hallmark of the Smolny-educated woman. It was that air of independence and confidence in her ability to hold her own in conversations with men that made such a woman the envy of European women everywhere, long before such liberated behavior had become widely acceptable in Western social circles. While studying in St. Petersburg she cultivated a talent for writing poetry in Russian and in her spare time she would write about the rocky loneliness of the beautiful Dalmatian coast of her homeland.

Tall and statuesque, with the typical dark-haired good looks of the Montenegrin royal family, it was while she was in St. Petersburg that she met and accepted the proposal of the then Prince of Naples, Victor Emanuele. Before they could marry it was necessary that she be converted from the Eastern Orthodox religion of Montenegro to the official Roman Catholic faith of Italy. In the Basilica of St. Nicholas at Bari, straight across the Adriatic from the Montenegrin seaport of Bar, she was baptized into her new faith. A few days later, on their wedding day, the joyous Romans lined the streets of the capital for miles and miles to celebrate the union of the royal couple. In 1900, Victor Emanuele III's father, King Umberto, was assassinated. Along side her husband, Elena ascended the Italian throne. With her background, she had little trouble in assuming her new role as Queen of Italy and in the years ahead would more than prove herself to the Italian people. The couple were very much in love and devoted to each other, even though she was considerably taller than he. It was said that the love match had been "cultivated" on his family's side in hopes of adding a bit of height to the Italian dynasty. King Nicholas of Montenegro became famous for aiding and abetting royal "love matches" for his daughters. Out of this union, four daughters and a son were born to Elena and Emanuele: Princess Giovanna, later to become Queen of Bulgaria; Princess Yolanda; Princess Mafalda, who, in the yet undreamed-of World War II, though of non-Jewish royal blood, would die behind the barbed wires of the German Buchenwald Nazi concentration camp; Maria, who would become the Princess of Bourbon; and Umberto II, who, in 1946, twenty-seven years hence, would reign for one month as King of Italy.

"Alfredo, bring His Highness and the Major some lunch and drink, as quickly as possible. Yes, just a little repast right now, then you shall go to bed. You must be deathly tired and should plan to sleep for as long as you wish. Food will be here in a minute.

"You have no idea how relieved I am to have you here. I have been worried sick about you. Ever since Father and Mother were detained in France and the rest of the family had left the country, I have been terribly concerned about your remaining back in Montenegro, the only one of us to stay back and continue the fight for freedom of Crna Gora. Italy is on our side and Victor would do anything he could to help; but, this, too, has become difficult. I imagine you know very little about what's been happening in the world, and in Italy."

Milo nodded, as the best meal he had seen since his days at St. Petersburg was placed in front of him, under a carved silver dome on an elaborate silver platter the likes of which could never be found in Montenegro.

"We know nothing about what is happening in the world. Our only connection to it was seeing your ships off the coast of Crna Gora, giving us hope, letting us know you knew we were still there fighting, and knowing there was an avenue of escape to safety should we ever need it; and we did."

At that point, Milo stopped talking and dived into the sumptuous meal before him, while, with a somber thoughtfulness, Her Majesty began to draw for her cousin a mental picture of a country, Italy, rendered impotent in its ability to develop and maintain a stable working government.

Italy had emerged from the war with a loss of 650,000 men, and an expenditure of fifteen billion dollars. The country of beautiful ruins, matchless scenery and brilliant musicians was also the country of the worst slums in Europe, mass illiteracy and great poverty. Five premiers in four years had left the government vulnerable to emerging Communist propaganda.

Moving into this vacuum came a man by the name of Benito Mussolini, a former Communist who had been expelled from the party when he joined the Italian army on the side of the Allies, and had now returned from the war a rabid nationalist, promoting a blind devotion to the great destiny that was to be Italy's.

"He is harsh and brutal; he does not care about the people. He struts around talking about the glory of Italy, when what he really means is the glory of Mussolini. I do not like what I hear nor see," her voice trailed off.

With a full and contented stomach, Milo's weariness could no longer be suppressed. He had fallen asleep, even as his beloved cousin spoke of the thunder clouds gathering on the horizon for the adopted country she ruled alongside her husband and had come to love as her own.

High above the sea on the rocky cliffs of Sorrento overlooking the Bay of Naples stood the Villa Tritone. The former American multi-millionaire, William Waldorf Astoria, now an English citizen and a Viscount, had bought the property from an Italian baron in the early 1900s and had brought to Sorrento some of the chic and international society he had cultivated during his years as Ambassador to Rome in the late 1800s. Of neoclassical lines, the villa revealed the remnants of a sixteenth century convent, its Romanesque and Moorish archaeological origins carrying through in the Mediterranean-style house and gardens. Now owned by the Count and Viscountess de Marchione, Queen Elena had arranged for her cousin to be invited for a visit, partially to give him a time of rest and relaxation in surroundings of peace and beauty so as to let rejuvination take place, as well as to remove him from the social and political crises hatching almost daily in Rome. Milo had had his share of revolutionary ferment in Russia and nationalistic fervors in Montenegro. Mussolini, having left the socialist party, currently was engaged in the founding of the fascist movement, organizing brigades of "Black Shirts" that swaggered around, destroying property of opponents, torturing or murdering the opposition, all in the name of nationalistic pride. Elena wanted her cousin away from the tension and social unrest increasing daily in the Eternal City.

Milo walked along the windswept balustrade of the promontory as the early morning fog burned off, leaving the seas below to glisten in the morning sun. Arches cut into the wall screening the garden from the bay below allowed one to peep through and see the descending steeply-staired streets carved into the rock with little alcoves placed at comfortable intervals for seating or viewing. Through tall cypresses to the left was a cathedral and across from it the piazza. At a distance, off to the other side, were the smaller villas, for generations the summer haunts of the intellectuals—poets, painters, writers, sculptors, patricians—and those who sought their company.

Warm breezes rippled through the trees and blew Milo's white linen jacket behind him as he took in the magnificent view of the palazzos in the hills, the mansions overlooking the bay, the winding Amalfi Drive along the perfect curves of the bay. Most of the monarchies of middle and southern Europe had been swept away by the winds of change that had blown at the close of the war; and although Italy had escaped that twelfth hour, she had come out of the war tormented by the over half million killed and more than one million wounded or disabled. She was further disillusioned by sharing considerably less generously in the fruits of her labor than did some of the other Allies. Although he had been sent away so as to be out of it, Milo recognized the signs and knew that Italy would soon be caught up by events of a future unknown and unseen, but equally as devastating for Elena as those he had just been through.

Being wined and dined by the Italian aristocracy was most certainly pleasurable. The Italian noblemen and women were impressed by the tall, handsome Montenegrin prince, a member of the same dynastic family as their queen, and one whose tales of valor and daring offered them good reason for holding their gorgeous fetes. Dancing under thousands of twinkling stars on marble verandas overlooking the moon-lit Mediterranean with gorgeously gowned beautiful women in his arms was not hard to take, but it was not now Milo's to take. His heart was in Crna Gora. His world had been turned upside down and he had been shaken out of it; but he was not ready to let it all go—his country, his heritage, his love.

After the passing of a couple of months of publicizing the plight of Montenegro while, at the same time, enjoying the hospitality of the Italian elegancia, Milo decided he must let no more time elapse before devoting his full-time efforts to obtaining the freedom of Montenegro. Certain maneuvers, though feeble, were underway in London to spur the Allied powers toward reconsidering the actions that had taken place against Montenegro. Milo began a letter writing campaign to the League of Nations.

He talked to everyone who would listen. There was nothing the Italian government could presently do to help him or Montenegro as it faced imminent dangers of its own from forces converging on each other from both the right and the left, threatening the very existence of the constitutional government and its parliamentary system.

In 1921 the news came from the French Riviera that King Nicholas of Montenegro had died. It was a sad moment Milo shared with Queen Elena as they bid her father good-by, after which Milo broke the news that he would be leaving Italy. Upon his departure she bestowed upon him a most gracious largesse Victor Emanuele III insisted he accept.

Two years later Mussolini entered Rome with his huge army of "Black Shirts". The King turned down the Cabinet's recommendation to declare a state of martial law, and instead, to keep peace, he asked Mussolini to take over the government, in return for which Mussolini promised the King he would respect the laws of the land and would immediately disband his "Black Shirts"—promises he had no intention of keeping. The national elections in 1924, sadly, did prove that the King had read public sentiment correctly; Mussolini's coalition received sixty-five percent of the total vote! Mussolini now was in a position to establish a totalitarian corporate state, which he quickly did, with himself symbolizing the state. The King was retained only as a figurehead, with Elena at his side, Queen in name only. Over night, Italy became a prison for all freedom-minded persons, as individual rights of any kind were drastically diminished or completely eliminated.

Chapultepec Palace stood with great dignity on the hill over-looking Mexico City. Ever since that day in June of 1864 when Archduke Maximilian, brother of Emperor Franz-Josef of Austria, and Maximilian's wife, Carlota, arrived to rule the country under the auspices of France's Napoleon, Mexicans had been wary of the intentions of the French. President Alvaro Obregon, who, as General of the Army, had driven the former President from power and from the city while he served as Commander of the military revolution that had been going on in Mexico since 1910, took great pleasure in welcoming the exiled Prince and Major Popovich to Mexico. The Mexican president was well aware that the former King and Queen of Montenegro had been held under virtual house arrest on the Riviera by the French right up to the day the King died, and that the French army had played a strong role backing the Serbs as they forced little Montenegro into the "Kingdom of United Slavs", or Yugoslavia as the new country would be called. To the Mexican President, this Prince without a country was a hero. Theirs was the same traitor; Obregon's own military actions had included waging guerrilla warfare against the French on Mexican soil, as Milo's had done on Montenegrin, so the two men had something in common. However, Obregon was now actively in the process of promoting new pacification policies to bring peace and stability to his war-wracked country, creating a national system of education and promoting a nationalistic renaissance in literature and the arts, while Milo, on the outside looking in, was a fish out of water, feeling just like what he was, a fugitive from the country he loved.

The Mexican government offered Mexico to Milo as his permanent home. Language would not have been a barrier as many in the higher levels of government and industry spoke French and German. But reports of revolutionary Communist activities kept surfacing so as to disquiet any temporary calm and negate any interest Milo might have been able to generate for Mexico to back international action on behalf of Montenegro. Secretary of the Interior of the United States, Albert B. Fall, was openly hostile to the Obregon regime, even as the United States Ambassador to Mexico Charles Warren was about to sign a final agreement between the Obregon regime and the United States. The warm welcome Prince Milo was receiving from the government might be masking a perception of usefulness on their part which could disappear overnight and leave him alone, embarrassed and defenseless, even though he felt Obregon himself was his friend. He could do nothing for Montenegro here, and so he left.

At the north end of the Bund sat Shanghai's Sasoon Cathay Hotel, reigning Queen of the Orient with its pyramidal roof and crystal penthouse suites. It was so European a city one could almost believe it was just outside the city limits of Paris, but China's great business establishments, the hongs or trading houses, lined the river embankment referred to as the Bund as opposed to the bookstalls and benches one would find beside meandering pathways under shady trees along the Seine. As an international business center run by British, French, American, White Russian and Jewish businessmen, there was nothing you couldn't buy in Shanghai and you could get away with anything, for a price. Decadence was her glittering mantle, savored by all who entered her port; her verve and irrepressible spirit never let her sleep, not even for a moment. Hundreds of opium dens and brothels co-existed right along side the magnificent mansions that were home to the rich and the lavish department stores that catered to every whim of the privileged classes. Tucked away in the golden dome atop the Hong Kong and Shanghai Bank was the home of the British Royal Air Force Club.

A large social colony, consisting mostly of the British, loved having garden parties, going to the Eiwo Racetrack, dining and dancing in the ballrooms of the many grand hotels and posh private clubs such as the Shanghai Club, which maintained running competition with The Raffles Hotel in Singapore for having the world's longest bar. The tall, handsome Prince was spotted quickly after his arrival at the Cathay Hotel and from that point on included in all the goings-on. It was sometime late in November of 1924, while dining with friends at the Astor Hotel, a fashionable hotel of somewhat worn-out grandeur, that he was introduced by his companion to an apparently highly popular, flirtatious woman by the name of Wallis Spencer, who was married to U.S. Navy flyer, Lt. Earl Winfield Spencer, Jr., stationed in Shanghai but nowhere around that evening. Not particularly beautiful, nor even pretty, a figure bony almost to the point of emaciation, she was, none-the-less, a lady of elegance, grace and witty intelligence. She had a way of making everyone feel good, and feel good about her. Noel Coward was part of this group and, like everyone else, reveled in the spirit of this "den of iniquity" that was Shanghai, which, four years later, right at that very hotel, provided the motivation for his "Private Lives." Obviously, the motivation was good; it took him all of four days to write it! This was all pretty heady stuff for the "Countryless Prince".

Civil War was exploding across China. In the Spring of 1925, China's left-wing leader, Sun Yat-sen, who had been the first president of the Republic of China since the abdication of the 268-year old Manchu dynasty in 1912, died. Everywhere there arose agitators stirring up workers and students, anti-foreign demonstrations in the streets, killings and other violent actions both in public places and behind the scenes. The Green Gang, a notorious criminal cartel under the direction of a man called Big-eared Tu, that dominated Chinese drug traffic through drugs, extortion and strong arm political tactics, was out to wrestle control from Sun Yat-sen's coalition and increase its own right-wing political power. Emerging into this political limelight came a man who was to leave his mark on the tapestry of China, Chiang Kai-shek, a soldier with an eye on climbing to the heights of power and wealth.

Because U.S. and British marines were on hand to protect

HOM

MY FATHER, THE PRINCE

their citizens, the international life of luxury and ease proceeded through all these crises without interruption. Three beautiful and famous sisters, the Soong sisters, with infinite grace and leverage of steel wielded total power throughout China. Their father, Charlie Soong, had financially backed the revolution of Dr. Sun Yat-sen, which led to the overthrow of the Manchu dynasty. One of Charlie Soong's daughters, Ching-ling, was married to Dr. Sun Yat-sen, a man old enough to be her father; the second daughter, May-ling, married Chiang Kai-shek, destined to become the next leader of China; and the third, Ai-ling, considered by many to be the brains behind the whole dynasty, married H.H. Kung (Kung Hsiang-hsi), a lineal descendant of Confucius, an extremely rich and powerful man.

Into Milo's new life of pleasurable, exotic and inconsequential demands came the beautiful, dewy-eyed, black-haired May-Yao Ching. Her distraction enticing and well-timed, her eagerness to pleasure in every possible way the tall, handsome Prince from another world partially made up for years of loneliness since Irena, so very long ago.

May-Yao Ching had recently returned from Great Britain where she had completed her university education. Her father was a Chinese banker, within the inner circle of H.H. Kung's business associates. Kung offered the Montenegrin prince a banking position, his knowledge of several languages - Russian, French, German and English, in addition to his native Serbian - most helpful in the banking world. The compensation would enable him to live in the style to which his title, but never his poor homeland, might entitle him.

There was no place in the world like Shanghai. Foreign and native coalitions operated freely, in great numbers, in every trade and with no restraint nor taxation. But in the factories, the back alleys, along the riverbeds, the other side of this coin of prosperity was hardly hidden from sight. Children, some less than ten years of age, worked as slaves in factories, sold upon the whim of the plant owner, left to die in the alleys, or their bodies tossed in the rivers.

To the north, Peking was gripped by terror and suspense. Rumors of plans for coup d' etats were abounding everywhere; seeking sanctuary in the Japanese Legation was a last frantic effort for the "Boy Emperor" after the British Legation refused him admission. None-the-less, Peking was the diplomatic center of China. Milo knew he did not want to stay indefinitely where he was and so decided to move on to the city to the north.

Because the railroad lines along a stretch out of Shanghai had been blown up, Milo traveled by ship to Tientsin, and from there by train to Peking. It was a miserable trip, first a voyage in rough seas, then a train trip with many breakdowns, little food, no toilets except a hole in the floor, a worry about bandits possibly stopping and entering the train to search and seize passengers of their inkling (whom Milo felt quite capable of handling considering his years in the mountains of Montenegro), and Chinese troops marching up and down everywhere. No bandits appeared, but whom did he run into getting off the train at Peking? None other than the charming U.S. naval officer's wife, Wallis Spencer.

Wallis was met at the station by a Navy car and when they realized they were both staying at the Grand Hotel de Pekin, she invited Milo to join her for the ride to the hotel.

"This may be presumptuous of me," stated Milo after they were underway, "but inasmuch as we have both just arrived and have not had anything to eat for many hours, perhaps after a little rest and a bit of freshening up, if you do not already have plans, you would be so kind as to join me for dinner tonight. I understand the food at the hotel is quite good."

"I would be delighted," she replied, looking at the handsome prince seated at her side with eyes that spoke of interest only thinly disguised.

"Good, then, eight o'clock, is that all right? We'll meet right here in the lobby," he said as the car pulled up in front of the hotel.

"Yes, that will be fine." He helped her out of the car as the driver took over directing the hotel servants regarding their luggage.

Moving toward the elevator after registering, the Prince heard a female voice call out, "Wallis, Wallis, I can't believe it's you, here in Peking."

Milo smiled to himself—the lady was a popular lady indeed.

Over a candlelight dinner that evening, Wallis and Milo talked about their lives and what had brought each of them to China. Amazingly open and frank, she said she was going to divorce her husband of about seven years; they had separated in the United States and this trip was sort of a last ditch effort at a reconciliation that was not working out. Leaving him with the Navy contingent in Shanghai and coming to Peking was the final nail in the coffin. The lady who had called out to her in the lobby was an old friend from the United States, now living with her husband in Peking. They had asked her to be their house guest for awhile, and she had accepted.

Would His Highness come to see her there? He assured her he would be delighted to do so; and he did, a number of times. They were never romantically entangled, perhaps because that same week she met a handsome naval attache to the Italian Embassy, a Luis de Cierro, who started right out actively wooing and courting Wallis. Like Milo, he had a passion for horses, so the two men found they had much in common, not to mention Milo's connection to the Italian royal family. During that winter, the Peking Horse Shows spotlighted the Italian participants and both Milo and Wallis were enthusiastic spectators. De Cierro, through the Italian Consulate where Mussolini's son was the Consul, let Mussolini know he had met a cousin of Queen Elena. Years later, the Italian dictator, as he sought during World War II to broaden his empire, would remember the chance meeting of one of his naval attaches half way around the world with a Montenegrin prince.

A fascinating international colony of businessmen and diplomats provided diversion for both Milo and Wallis during these days but in different ways and for awhile these were happy times for both of them, later to be remembered by each as a peaceful interlude in lives that were tentatively "on hold". Wallis' personal and romantic life was in turmoil, while Milo's very existence was fragile and seemingly meaningless. A Prince without a country, a man without a family, a human being alone on the landscape of life with another revolution fomenting all around him.

On January 3, 1925, Mussolini declared himself Dictator of Italy. Milo decided to leave Peking and return to Europe, while the Navy Lieutenant's wife went back to Shanghai. Neither could possibly imagine then that another prince of even higher royal status would enter her life, resulting in the greatest monarchy in the world dropping to its knees. Milo and Wallis always remained friends; they would meet again one day, in another time and another place, and under very different circumstances.

Driving through Cernobbio in the spectacular lake district of Northern Italy on the tree-shaded road about twenty-five miles northeast of Milan, the Villa d'Este suddenly looms up before one as a luminous pearl surrounded by a wreath of splendorous flowers. Elegant rows of towering cypresses lead down steps toward the often fog-shrouded Lago d'Como, while mountain streams ripple over rocks from the high hills behind the world-famous hotel, winding their way amongst the poplars, beeches, elms, pines, cedars, chestnut and palm trees.

The history of the noble origins of this palace-hotel dates back four centuries. First known as the Villa Garrovo, it was purchased in 1815, by Caroline of Brunswick, the Princess of Wales, and renamed the New Villa d'Este, "New" to differentiate it from the Villa d'Este in Tivoli. The "New" was soon dropped. The Princess bought the Villa d'Este as a sort of personal Royal Palace, away from England and the husband who had neglected her for many years, but who was destined someday to ascend the British throne as King George IV with Caroline at his side as his Queen. For now, though, for her private Italian palace she ordered massive restoration and redecoration; the best architects and painters of Italy, taking their inspiration from Greek mythology, added new wings, and even a theatre, to the original building, while magnificent frescoes and priceless statues were erected in the halls and outside in the gardens. She was loving and kind to the hired servants and local people of Cernobbio, and overly generous; she treated them as if they were her family.

During this time a gentleman by the name of Bartolomeo Pergami was introduced to her by General and Countess Pino, the couple from whom she had purchased the Villa. Caroline offered Pergami the position of Courier for her travels, but soon elevated him to her Chamberlain and gave him the title of Baron, while his sister, Countess Oldi, became Caroline's Lady-in-waiting. Unfortunately, the Princess's pursuit of luxury and benefaction of the arts were totally out of proportion to her means and as a result, she wound up in debt to her banker in Rome, the Prince Torlonia, and was finally forced to deed her beautiful palace over to him as collateral for the money she owed. More serious, however, was that news of her activities and adventures with Pergami had reached across the Channel and discredited her as a woman fit to be the future Queen of England. As her husband sought to commence divorce proceedings in England, she moved from the Villa d'Este to a smaller residence in Pensaro facing the valley of the Foglia River. Before the legal proceedings had actually gotten underway, her father-in-law, King George III, died. She left Italy for England, fully expecting to assume her role, alongside her husband, as Queen of England; but what awaited her was a futile year-long fight in the House of Lords for her place on the throne. On the day of the coronation ceremony, the doors of Westminster Abbey were closed in her face. Two weeks later, humiliated and depressed, Caroline died, never to see her beloved Villa d'Este again.

Prince Domenico Orsini bought the fabled place from Prince

Torlonia, then after awhile sold it to the Baron Ippolito Ciani. The Baron brought another monarch to the Villa d'Este, the Empress Maria Feodorovna, Czarina of Russia for thirty years and widow of Czar Nicholas I. Her son, Alexander II, was Emperor and Russia and the Imperial Court were enjoying a period of peace and happiness, leaving Maria feeling free to leave the icy winters of her country for the beauty and sunshine of the Northern Italian lake district. A two month lease of the property turned into a two year stay. Day and night the little town of Cernobbio bubbled with gaiety and enjoyment. Cossacks on horseback were brought in to stand guard at the Villa gates, while satin-lined, richly decorated coaches carried Grand Dukes, Princes, foreign and Italian diplomats around Cernobbio and Lake Como. Then the Czarina was called home to the Imperial Palace at St. Petersburg. The wonderful life at the Villa, the exotic atmosphere of the partially Oriental Russian culture, slightly barbarian in its effect as remnants of damage to the furniture and gardens would attest, ended. The Villa became lonely and silent.

In 1873, the heirs of the Baron Ciani, numerous in number, joined together with the Mayor of Milan, to form a limited company for the purpose of acquiring the entire property, along with another famous hotel close by, the Hotel de la Reine d'Angleterre. Thus the Villa d'Este rose again, its accumulated fame through the centuries intact, from Renaissance to Rococo, in the sunshine or in the shadows, still one of the most beautiful monuments to the combined efforts of Man and Nature ever built.

To this harbor of beauty and tranquility arrived Prince Milo in 1926 for the indulgence of a lifetime, the opening of the Villa d'Este Golf Club at Montorfano. King Victor Emanuele III and Queen Elena of Italy used the opening as an excuse to escape the oppressive Fascist government controlling all of Italy, as well as offer Elena an opportunity to see her beloved cousin again. This was the end of Milo's wanderings, his last hurrah. Ahead of him lay a new world, a new life. There would be no returning to the old, ever.

7 | A New Life

Prince Milo arrived on British soil broke and destitute. The governments of the countries he had visited had offered him permanent residency; men of privilege and power had offered him prestige positions with their companies, but all these countries were in the midst of their own political turmoils and their leaderships were in no position to think about helping some tiny, foreign kingdom tucked away in a remote part of Europe. Milo had dedicated his life to obtaining the independence of his native land, whether or not the Montenegrin people would want the monarchy restored or not was not germane to his goal. He could not let himself be locked into a situation that closed the door on his continuing his life's work.

Bounded on the north by Euston Road, on the east by Southampton Row, on the south by New Oxford Street and on the west by Tottenham Court Road sat the Bloomsbury section of London, with its old Georgian terraces and squares and tree-lined parks surrounded by iron fences and gateways leading to well-placed benches on which to sit. In the 1920s, in and around these squares clustered "The Bloomsbury Set", young, attractive Londoners of unusual talent, artists and writers dedicated to changing the world and in many cases succeeding admirably in achieving some of their own unique goals. Virginia Woolf and her writer-editor husband, Leonard, lived there at the time, in the basement of a building famous for being where, two hundred years prior, William Hogarth, an engraver of satirical pictures of 18th Century England and inventor of the press which bore his name, had lived. Milo took a room in the basement of a building near-by, not quite so fancy, at No. 44 Bedford Square. Three floors above resided the hopefully-fashionable London hostess, Lady Ottoline Morrell. She simply adored holding soirees for various members of the "Bloomsbury Set", but Milo wasn't invited; she didn't know he existed, down below her, below street level.

Forced to accept any sort of menial work that came along in order to support himself, eventually Milo landed a job as assistant to the cashier at a small, local branch of the Bank of England. His knowledge of foreign exchange and foreign languages proved to be the door-opener and within a few months he was transferred to the London branch in Knightsbridge, where his title and handsome good looks were an added qualification. Just before he moved, Lady Morrell "discovered him" and he was invited to one of her parties!

Settling himself into a tiny flat at the outskirts of Knightsbridge and feeling comfortable in his new position with the bank, Milo started to look for some outside diversions. He wasn't overly happy with his job but it enabled him to pay the bills as well as make the acquaintance of important people in London's business and social circles. London's small Montenegrin Society Club discovered him and this offered him a sponsorship and platform from which to promulgate his message about Montenegro's freedom.

One evening, Yanko Brajovitch, one of the most famous sculptors in all of Europe, as well as a Montenegrin soldier and statesman of note who had survived the war and its devastating aftermath only to be sentenced to three years in a Serbian prison on the horrendous charges of being a Montenegrin patriot, was exhibiting his beautiful pieces at The Royal Academy of Arts in Piccadilly. Sponsored by the Montenegrin Society Club, Prince Milo was asked to be the specially honored guest for the evening.

The chandelier glistened brightly above the heads of the

HOM

distinguished guests milling around in the reception hall of the Academy, its lights illuminating the pale green damask walls that were a perfect foil for the marble busts and figure-sized statues on display. Included was a figure of Christ standing with upflung arms in an appeal to nations to cease their strife, already being acclaimed as an ecclesiastical masterpiece in its own time. It had been sent over from Paris for this one last exhibition prior to its being placed permanently in the Hall of the League of Nations.

As Mr. Brajovitch finished up acknowledging the acclaim of the assembly, he dropped his voice and said, "Now my country is practically a slave of Serbia. Montenegro, the smallest nation of Europe, who for five hundred years beat back the swarm of Turkish Islam, entered the war on the side of the Allied armies, yet lost her independence through her friends. The story of Montenegro is the blackest page in the history of the Allied armies. With us here, to be honored this evening, is its most valiant and worthy hero, His Highness, Prince Milo, the man, who, in my opinion, should be its next King."

After a few remarks extolling the urgency of bringing all possible pressure to bear for the freeing of Montenegro from Yugoslavia, Milo greeted the guests who formed a long line to personally meet him. Among them was one Lady Doreen Powell, an aristocratic blonde lady, bedecked in jewels and ermine, with piercing green eyes and an imperious personality, who insisted on staying right at his side, talking all the while. Milo found it difficult to greet everyone and still give the attention to this lady that she seemed to expect. Then a hat caught his eye. Had she not had it on, he probably would never have noticed her. But she did, and he did.

A one-inch navy-blue grosgrain ribbon encircled the edge of the wide brim on the cream-colored straw hat, streamers cascading down the back of its wearer. In front, to the left, a pale pink rose lay atop the brim over a pleating of cream-colored netting. Below, on a graceful, slender female form was a sleeveless, three-quarter length chiffon dress combining multi-hues of pale blues, pinks, and various shades of cream, sashed in at the waist and bowed with the identical navy-blue grosgrain ribbon. Two long strands of pearls showed off the swanlike neck that led right back up to the face with the most extra-ordinarily luminous sky-blue eyes he had ever seen. His gaze stopped there. Excusing himself momentarily from the receiving line and from Lady Powell, much to her consternation, he moved toward the lady in the hat. Weaving his way through the crowd he kept his eyes riveted on the vision in front of him: "the delicate, slender structure of bone, the face mesmerizing by its almost ethereal quality that combined expressions of love, wonderment, and kindness, all framed by dark brown curls peering from underneath the wide-brimmed hat against a porcelain white skin that seemed to actually blush with each breath taken.

Quiveringly holding a cup of tea in one hand, a saucer in the other, all the while balancing a beaded white handbag dangling by a gold chain from one arm, she was giving undivided attention to what the man next to her was saying. They were looking at the icons from an old Montenegrin monastery that were in the case in front of them. Was she with him, or had she come alone? He knew he wanted to meet her, and as guest of honor this, of course, should not be too difficult.

As he came closer, they stopped talking and looked in his direction.

"Good evening. May I present myself? I am Prince Milo of Montenegro."

"Oh, yes, Your Highness, I know, of course. I am honored to meet you. I am Helena Smith. And this is——." She turned to ask the name of the gentleman she had been speaking to so as to introduce him but he had slipped away through the crowd.

"I hope I'm not intruding on anything."

"Oh, no. I don't even know the gentleman's name. We were admiring the icons from your country. They are lovely. In fact, the whole exhibit is wonderful. Your country must be very beautiful. You have every reason to be proud of it."

"Thank you for your kind words. I admit I think so, and so do about 500,000 Montenegrins." About that time he was thinking to himself that something else was quite beautiful, too. She was not a beauty in the true sense of the word; under the magnetic sky-blue eyes was a straight, classic nose and a serene mouth that conveyed intelligence and wisdom. All three, he would later come to know, she possessed in great abundance. Her voice, a perfect English, void of any accent whatsoever, prompted him to ask, "Are you English, or——?"

"Yes, I am," she replied, "however, for the past fourteen years I have lived in the United States. I am here on vacation."

"I see. Then you'll be returning to America?"

She nodded.

"I am sorry. I had hoped to get to know you a little better. Perhaps——" he hesitated, then continued, "you'd be willing to have tea with me some afternoon, if you have time before you leave."

Her eyes popped wide open. "I would be delighted."

As they made arrangements to meet, he realized this was the first lady he had ever been so instantly totally attracted to. What was it? Why? It didn't matter; he had already made up his mind about her.

Bleak but ruggedly beautiful, the Yorkshire moors in the midlands of England are an irresistible lure for all admirers of the three famous Bronte sisters—Emily, author of "Wuthering Heights"; Charlotte, author of "Jane Eyre"; and Anne, also a novelist and poet of talent—and their brother, Branwell, the city drunk who made the Black Bull Hotel and Pub famous. Just off the steep, winding, coblestone Main Street of the tiny village of Haworth, background for the Bronte legacy and site of "Wuthering

Heights", lying on the outskirts of the town of Keighley, Grace Helena Smith was born, six years later than the Prince. A Yorkshire wood-turner's daughter, she attended the Keighley Girls' Grammar School, always placing first in "the Form", or occasionally second, when her sister, Edith, placed first. To try to carve out a better life for themselves and their daughters, her parents had migrated to America with the two girls while they were still in their early teens. Her sister and Mother had died, and this was Helena's first trip back to her native land.

In the days that followed Milo and Helena met almost daily— dining at some charming, quiet, out-of-the-way restaurant; driving to the country, perhaps to Stratford-upon-Avon in Warwickshire to catch the current play at the Royal Shakespeare Theatre; viewing the tennis championships at Royal Albert Hall at Kensington Gore; enjoying a symphony by the Royal Philharmonic Symphony Orchestra at the Royal Festival Hall on the South Bank; or just spending an afternoon wandering hand in hand through the Victoria and Albert Museum. No woman had quite caught his fancy such as this before. Quite plainly, he found himself falling in love. She already had.

He followed her back to America and in 1927 by the magnificent California shores of the Santa Barbara coastline they were married. A year later a baby girl was born and they named her Milena, after the last Queen of Montenegro. When friends asked where the unusual name came from they were told it was made up from the first part of Milo's name and the last part of Helena's name. Their neighbors thought Milo was a starving author (he had recently completed writing a book, "The Extinction of Montenegro"). Later they would learn he was really a starving prince.

Continuing his efforts to gain his country's freedom, in December of 1928, Milo held a press conference for the purpose of publicizing a letter he had written to the Council of the League of Nations, hoping to plead the case for his country's independence in front of the entire world. In the interview, he told the reporters that The League of Nations had actually been bombarded with appeals for adjudication of the Montenegrin question, but that not only had it totally ignored the matter, it had prevented any news from leaking out that it had ever received any such appeals. France, one of the most powerful League nations, having been a supporter of Serbia in its conquest of Montenegro, was determined to prevent any information whatsoever from being released regarding Montenegro's plight. On Sunday, December 30, 1928, the "Los Angeles Times" ran its article about Prince Milo's press conference under the banner, "League Scored by Royal Exile"; over a photo of Prince Milo was the caption, "Prince Challenges Action of Powers". Sub-headings included such statements as: "Once Prince of Montenegro Works for Nation", "France Blamed for Letting Serbia Control", "Patriot Declares Protests Kept in Dark".

It was right about that time Milo learned that Alvaro Obregon, who had just been re-elected President of Mexico, had been shot and killed by a young fanatic. An understanding friend was gone.

Everywhere political conditions seemed to be in a state of constant upheaval. 1929 began with chilling economic winds blowing across many countries, generating conditions that would soon send violent ripples throughout the world. On January 5th, Serbian King Alexander of Yugoslavia declared himself Dictator because of internal disorders revolving around Croatian nationalistic dissatisfaction. (Almost seventy years later, this conflict still had not been resolved.) Milo could not let himself be deterred from his task; he must press onward, no matter what the consequences.

In San Francisco, The Committee for the Freedom and Independence of Montenegro, small, active, but very strapped for money, tried to publish monthly an official pamphlet for

Montenegrin loyalists, "The Montenegrin Mirror", for the purpose of publicizing and promoting the cause of liberty. Prince Milo's book was printed serially over a several month period. Near-by in Palo Alto, the Chancellor of Stanford University, David Starr Jordan, a friend of Montenegro, took up the cause and spoke frequently about how miserably it had been treated by the Allies after World War I.

There were those who knew and understood. They spoke out, but their voices were a lonely cry in the wilderness. Although pleased to see these efforts on behalf of Montenegro, Milo began thinking that he could do more good in Europe, so that summer, he bid his lovely wife and baby daughter a sad good-bye, promising to bring them over as soon as possible. Possible never came.

London in the early 1930s was a city that had left the hectic gaieties of the 20s and its emotional release after World War I and was treading a more somber path through the depression years, years which were destined to lead to a newer and even greater wartime scenario in the not too distant future. Upon the Prince's return to Great Britain, Lady Doreen Powell quickly returned to his side. Widowed by a rich nobleman a number of years previous, and quite a few years Milo's senior, her gestures of friendship, nevertheless, were appreciated and most graciously accepted by the poverty-ridden Prince. She helped His Highness find a small but nice flat in the elite Grosvenor section of London. It was while visiting some of the smaller London auction houses that the idea came to Milo to deal in antiques as an income producing activity, with Lady Powell as his partner. His plan was to purchase the items for his own use in his flat and then after a period of time sell them, individually, at a profit. Because she would be financing the purchases, upon sale, she, of course, would receive her money back first, plus interest or an appropriate share of the profit. It proved to be an idea whose time had come; for the rest of his life this was the way he made his living. After a few years he no longer needed to borrow from Lady Doreen. Their friendship, nevertheless, remained close until her death many years later.

Soon the large houses of Sotheby's and Christie's became part of his habitat. He enjoyed wandering through their numerous rooms and floors of displays—furniture, objects' d art, china, crystal, silver, gold, paintings—the latter two became his specialties, and over a period of time, he acquired the knowledge and appraisal expertise necessary to be considered somewhat of an expert in these areas. At the same time, he did not neglect the smaller, lesser known antique shops of Mayfair or those on Regent or Bond Streets.

With the passage of but a few months Prince Milo's flat developed a beautifully Victorian air, elegantly furnished with exquisite antiques, hand painted on finely polished woods; lovely vermeil and porcelain pieces to enchant the eye; old Persian rugs, if a bit worn, non-the-less homey; and quite a number of paintings of a grand scale on the walls. There were several vitrines throughout the downstairs rooms displaying small objects' d art, some Russian eggs, his numerous Montenegrin medals, and a collection of 18th Century French fans, figurines and cameos.

The Prince and his Lady spent many hours together, at Claridges, the Connaught, the Savoy, or the Ritz, taking high tea or dining with some of his new, admiring friends. They frequented the restaurants and theatres at Piccadilly Circus; enjoyed The Royal Opera of Covent Garden; took in the Royal Ascot Race Meeting, that rarefied institution founded in 1711 where their attendance in the Royal Enclosure was reported in the society section of the venerable Tatler Magazine; as well as the Derby at Epsom Race Course in Surrey. She helped him select a few suits on Savile Row, some accessories at Garrard or Asprey Jewelers, and various miscellaneous items for home or person at Harrod's. Life was pleasant, indeed.

His new friends, never neglecting, of course, to call ahead of time, enjoyed dropping by his beautifully furnished flat for afternoon tea. One day as he was greeting some guests at the front door he happen to glance down the street as a car pulled up to the curb. A lady alighted from it and entered a flat—it was the lady from Shanghai, 1924. Then, Wallis Warfield Spencer, she was now Wallis Warfield Simpson. Her second husband was Ernest Simpson, a partner in the firm of Simpson, Spence and Young, shipping merchants. Inviting the couple to have tea with him one summer afternoon, Milo found Wallis still the interesting, witty, spirited conversationalist, the lady of grace and charm he remembered from their days in China five years ago. Ernest Simpson was a wealthy businessman from "the old school" so to speak, perhaps somewhat nondescript but well-read, cultured and gracious. It would be only a couple more years till an event would take place that would call upon him to muster every ounce of graciousness he had within him, while, at the same time, the course of a nation would be changed forever, with Wallis' name permanently inscribed in the annals of history.

A few months elapsed getting settled and adapting to his new life, then Milo decided it was time he got back to focusing on his goal—gaining the freedom of Montenegro. Joining with him in his efforts were his good friend, Major Marko Popovitch, past Commander of the Royal Guard of Montenegro; Luigi Criscuolo, Founder of the Committee for Montenegrin Independence in New York and holder of the Knight Grand Cross of the Order of Danilo I; and Jovan Ciubranovitch, Member of the Directorate of the Montenegrin National Defense League, headquartered in Geneva, Switzerland, among others. They spoke to clubs and groups, wrote pamphlets and news articles, gave interviews and press conferences, and in general, spent the next few years of their lives carrying the banner for Montenegro's independence.

The London "Daily Telegraph" became interested in the case of the little Balkan country. On August 29, 1930, the

HOM

newspaper published a Letter to the Editor from Paul Popovitch, Ex-Montenegrin Minister Plenipotentiary, headlined, "Montenegro's Plight", which outlined the solemn war assurances of the Allies and their promises for her independence. A day later, the same newspaper carried another letter, also headlined "Montenegro's Plight", by Major H.C.C. Gibbings, of the 1st Royal Inniskilling Fusiliers, Junior United Service Club, about the loss of Montenegro's independence. The following year the "London Express" took up the gauntlet and ran articles during a period of time the Four Power Conference was holding its meetings in London, hoping to bring their attention to the tragedy that had befallen Montenegro. Major Gibbings again followed-through with another one of his letters. Continuing its interest in the beleaguered nation, in March of that year the newspaper published an article about Prince Milo, their headline referring to him as "The King Without a Throne", with subtitles under it, "Prince Milo of Montenegro in London", "Balkan War Cloud" and "A Nation with Two Rifles per Man". Should be enough to get anyone's attention!

The leading organization representing exiled Montenegrins in Great Britain, The British Friends of Montenegro, were pleased to learn that a newly formed branch of The Royalist International, at its second meeting, passed a resolution of sympathy with the deposed monarchs of Montenegro and Austria, Hungary and Croatia. Prince Milo was delighted to attend a meeting to thank them, on behalf of all exiled Montenegrins, for their support.

September 9th, 1932, found Milo going further afield for a week's stay at Lethendry Lodge, Grantown, Scotland, to enlist support for his country's freedom. The aspirations of Montenegro and His Highness's desire to serve his countrymen again were well reported by the news media.

In December of that year he traveled to Geneva, Switzerland, where he pleaded the case of Montenegro to every member of the League of Nations who would listen. They nodded, shook their heads in sympathy, but felt it was a "fait accompli". It was from there that Milo sent his patriotic and beautiful holiday message to all Montenegrins and Montenegrin sympathizers everywhere, printed in both Serbo-Croatian and English, with the crest of the Country of Montenegro and the House of Petrovic-Njegoš at the top.

He continued on. But no freedom and independence for Montenegro.

1933, and mankind's greatest cataclysm to date was commencing to unfold. In the Near East, Japan moved into Manchuria, ostensibly to have a strategic base for operations against the Russians, but immediately commenced active aggression against China. Adolph Hitler was named Chancellor of Germany and the Nazi party, adopting severe anti-Jewish measures, quickly locked the country in its grip. 1934 saw rising tension enveloping many nations as they scrambled to form mutual defense alliances and sign worthless non-aggression pacts, some looking for guarantees of peace, others looking for a piece of this and a piece of that. Once again, a fortune-teller prophesied the assassination of another Serbian king, but this time it would be a Karageorgevich. On October 9th, King Alexander of Yugoslavia, a grandson of King Nicholas of Montenegro, and son of Princess Zorka of Montenegro and King Peter of Serbia, was murdered in Marseilles, France, by a Macedonian revolutionary—another country that had been forced into becoming part of Yugoslavia showing its resentment. Somehow Hungary got the blame for having masterminded it so nobody bothered look further for the underlying cause of the assassination. No one saw that Yugoslavia was a country not meant to be. In December of 1934, fighting broke out between Italian and Ethiopian troops near the frontier between Ethiopia and Italian Somaliland, while elsewhere that same year, the very married Mrs. Wallis

Warfield Simpson met the very unmarried Prince of Wales, heir to the British throne. By 1935, theirs was the romance of the century.

1936 was a year of tremendous upheavals, both within the British Isles and on the continent. It commenced on January 19th with the death of King George V of England; the Prince of Wales was now King Edward VIII. Wallis, at his insistence, remained ever at his side in front of the world, as scandals about their private lives swirled around them, including possible illicit connections with the Nazis and fraternization with Mussolini. In the summer of that year the English Press was put on strict censorship not to even mention Wallis' name anymore, but newspapers and magazines from the continent continued coverage of the most exciting love affair since Anthony and Cleopatra. After her interlocutory decree of divorce was granted in October, to become final in six months, the King of England presented her with her engagement ring, a magnificent Cartier emerald. During this time he entertained much at the Palace, Wallis always his hostess. And Wallis, herself, gave many small dinners at her flat. There was one before the summer holiday when she and the King were to vacation along the Dalmatian coast aboard a chartered yacht, the "Nahlin", that Prince Milo was invited to. He was asked to tell them about Montenegro. He spoke proudly of the beautiful country he had to forsake and assured them they would be greeted warmly there. True to his word, peasants from remote Montenegrin villages came down to cheer the famous lovers as the "Nahlin" pulled into Bay of Kotor one sunny afternoon.

On May 9th, 1936, Italy officially annexed Ethiopia to Italian Somaililand and Eritrea, all now called Italian West Africa. Mussolini staged a victory celebration in Rome, boasting, "At last, Italy has her empire, a civilizing empire, humanitarian towards all the people of Ethiopia." Milo was invited to the Eternal City to attend the celebration and to see and hear his cousin and her husband proclaimed Emperor and Empress of Ethiopia.

The new Emperor and Empress contributed their gold wedding bands to a nationwide collection which was being held to help defray the expenses of war incurred in forming this new "civilizing empire". Throughout the world a photograph run by Wide World News immortalized the moment. Germany, Austria and Hungary immediately recognized the conquest; one year later Britain and France followed suit. Ethiopia's Emperor Haile Selassie had to flee in exile to England, the most recent in an ever-growing list of past and future royal exiles. A dejected Milo could only wonder what was next, and did not consider it an honor when, back in England toward the end of the month, he received an overseas telegram, to wit:

SSS Roma
S A Principe Milo di Montenegro
    Ringraziando V A R Parte Presa al giubilo popolo italiano prego gradire espressione sentimenti deferenti
            Cordiali 1 Mussolini

(Thanking your Royal Highness for the part taken in the celebration of the Italian people. Please accept the expression of my cordial and respectful sentiments.
            Mussolini)

Suppression is called celebration?
That October, Mussolini met with Hitler at Berchtesgaden and together the two tyrants reached a secret agreement aligning the foreign policies of the two countries.
The fateful day came when Prime Minister Baldwin of England had to bluntly tell the His Majesty, King Edward VIII, that there was no way the Cabinet Ministers would ever approve his marrying a divorced woman, who would then become Queen of England. As King, he was head of the Church of England which did not condone remarriage after divorce under any circumstances. The wife of the head of the Church could not be in

145

HOM

violation of Church doctrine. At 10:00 p.m. on the evening of December 10th, 1936, while Wallis Warfield Simpson was in France, Milo, along with the rest of the world, listened spellbound as King Edward VIII of England declared his inability to carry the heavy duties and responsibilities of his position without the help and support of the woman he loved, and with those words he abdicated the throne of England. Milo remembered the times together, in Shanghai and Peking, and tea at his flat in London, Wallis and he. How fragile the monarchies, even the strongest.

It was about this time Milo faced up to the futility of his efforts. Montenegro had been absorbed into Yugoslavia, and in his eighteen years of efforts absolutely nothing had occurred to change that fact. He decided it was time to stop hanging onto what appeared to be no more and start making a new life for himself. As for the wife and daughter he had left half way around the world, he had stopped thinking much about them long ago.

In January, 1937, Mussolini conquered Albania and "set up" Victor Emanuele III and Elena as King and Queen of Albania! They're now King and Queen of three countries, in name only, in effect prisoners in their palaces, while in France on June 3rd, the former King of England, the Duke of Windsor, married Wallis Simpson, the world looked on, making her his Duchess. It was only one month later, on the other side of the globe, another famous woman made further history, unfortunately, this time tragically; the celebrated American aviatrix, Amelia Earhart, first woman to fly solo across the Atlantic, disappeared over the South Pacific. The riveting news of these entirely different women held the world's attention as it vainly sought any diversion from acknowledging the storm clouds rapidly gathering on the horizon.

That year both Austria and Czechoslovakia fell beneath the German yoke; in 1938 Poland; whereupon, on September 3, 1939, Britain, France, Australia, New Zealand and India declared war on Germany. World War II had arrived. That same day a German U-boat sank the British passenger liner, "Athenia", with 1,400 passengers on board; 316 Americans lost their lives. Two days later the United States declared its neutrality! A couple of months later that declaration was amended, then withdrawn. By then, Russia and Finland were at war, which led to Russia's expulsion from the League of Nations.

Evacuations from London began. At this point Milo felt totally devastated by and disengaged from the world around him.

In Spring of 1940, Germany conquered Denmark and Norway, followed by Belgium and Holland; then they regrouped for the conquest of France. In June, Italy entered the war on the side of Germany and invaded southern France, while four members of the Balkan Entente—Yugoslavia, Rumania, Greece and Turkey—declared their neutrality. By June 25th, France surrendered. Now for the Battle of Britain. London became the target for a tremendous aerial bombardment, when on September 15th, 1,000 German bombers and 700 fighters swept over the city in wave after wave, but the British spirit did not falter and soon the tide turned. On September 27, 1940, a three-power pact was concluded by Berlin, Rome and Tokyo, each party pledging the others aid for ten years, but with Japan not having to commit herself to go to war against Britain or her allies. Thus the "Axis" officially came into being. By the end of October, the British RAF had won the Battle of Britain, 1,733 German planes shot down to 915 British. Germany stopped its daylight raids, but around the 15th of November picked up its nighttime ones. The "Blitz" had begun. By the end of May, 1941, over 43,000 Britishers would be killed and 51,000 more seriously injured.

In March of 1941, under German pressure, Yugoslavia's Regent, Prince Paul Karageorgevich, reluctantly agreed to join the Axis alliance, only to be overthrown by patriotic anti-German elements within the country. So much for Yugoslavian neutrality! The German and Italian Second Armies then invaded and, in short shrift, overthrew Yugoslavia. Two resistance movements arose within the country: the Chetniks, operating out of

Serbia and Montenegro; and the Partisans, operating out of other parts of the country. The trouble was the Chetniks and the Partisans hated each other more than they hated the enemy, and as a result, a bloody three-way war raged in Yugoslavia. The Yugoslavs couldn't get together even to fight a common enemy, but they did give the Axis a run for their money; and in the end, the Partisans became a major force in routing the Axis out of Yugoslavia. At this point, Germany and Italy split up control of the area, with Italy taking part of Slovenia, the Dalmatian coast, Montenegro, and the Adriatic Islands, while Germany took Croatia, Serbia and other inland portions. Mussolini wanted to declare Montenegro independent, "under Italian protection", restore the monarchy, "under Italian protection", and thereby establish a situation similar to Italy, a monarchy where he was the dictator. The throne was offered to Prince Michael Petrovic-Njegoš, grandson of the former King Nicholas of Montenegro; he wisely rejected the honor. Later, in 1944, Michael was arrested by the Nazi Gestapo for being "uncooperative" and deported to Germany until the end of the war. He died in 1986 at age 77 in Paris, where his son, Nicolas, an architect, lives today. The next to be offered the throne was a more distant member of the Montenegro's former royal family, Prince Milo, More distant in location, also, safe in England, he, too, promptly turned the offer down. Nazi Germany, in the meantime, made Croatia into a separate puppet state in the Balkans, "under Italian protection", a fateful decision for one Andrija Artukovic, who was Croatia's Minister of Interior, Justice and Religion. In 1986, after having lived in the United States for over forty years, at age 86, he was extradited from California to Yugoslavia where he was tried, convicted and sentenced to death for running two dozen concentration camps in Croatia, where 700,000 to 900,000 Jews, Serbians and gypsies were tortured and murdered during the time he held that Ministerial position. Bad blood has run deep between Serbia and Croatia for many generations; it still does.

Despite a 1939 non-aggression pact, Hitler attacked the

Soviet Union on June 22, 1941, but it took until December 5th, almost six months later, for a Russian counterattack to get underway. Two days after it did, half way around the world, on December 7th, Japan attacked the United States naval base in Hawaii. The United States declared a state of war the next day, and for this it took the Axis only three days to return the declaration of war on the United States. All the players were now on the field for World War II.

Bombs were now falling on London day and night, leaving the city almost totally demolished. Still feeling the ravages of those former years of war in which he had fought so bravely and so fruitlessly, Milo decided to leave London for a smaller city, one not in the eye of the storm. Dublin, Ireland, a city much like London but in miniature, had remained almost exactly as it had been when Joyce, Yeats and Behan lived there. One of the more civilized of European cities, horns only infrequently sounded in anger, harsh words were rarely uttered whether when spoken in a rather musical English or an ancient Gaelic. To ask directions would often mean being escorted personally to your destination. Sitting astride the Liffey River, Dublin is a city built on a manageable scale; the average person can climb to the top of most structures and most destinations can be reached by walking. There on Grafton Street Milo took a room at the elegant Shelbourne Hotel as he looked for a permanent residence for himself, not to be too far from the exclusive shops, elegant restaurants, and famous pubs lining Grafton Street between St. Stephen's Green and 400 year-old Trinity College.

During the reign of George the III, block after block of gracious brick row houses had been built. Milo bought a two-story Georgian home on Arranmore Road in a nice section of Dublin, its simple brick facade enlivened by white stone cornices and trim, highlighting twin columns capped by fan windows framing

149

a forest green door. A car was next on the agenda and he purchased a Daimler, the car of the British royal family. Meanwhile,
Lady Doreen Powell had settled in at Harcourt Terrace, less
than a mile away. Being of half Irish, half English ancestry, she
was not unhappy about following the Prince to Ireland. She had
many friends there whom she would introduce to him, and
whether during war times or peace, life moved at a more lei-
surely pace, pleasing to both of them.

The crystal chandelier gleamed over the elegantly-set table
in the dining room at Harcourt Terrace. It was October 3rd, the
Prince's birthday, and Lady Doreen had invited fifty or so of
Dublin's notables and sociables to meet His Highness and help
celebrate his birthday. Gilt-edged paper inside her leather-bound
hostess book, with its moire silk inside covers and silk ribbon
marker, described the table plan, the menu, wine list, the hostess's
dress and jewelry, and the names of all the guests—a lasting
momento of the evening for His Highness.

The flickering fire in the white marble fireplace emitted a
welcoming glow as guests were greeted in the drawing room and
offered an aperitif of choice. A solid mahogany arch-top mantel
clock was centered over the fireplace with brass lion heads set
on either side; above the mantle hung a large, gold-framed, oil
painting of the hunt, depicting the chase of the elusive foxes that
roam the Irish countryside. As later-arriving guests entered, the
early-arrivals flowed over into the mahogany-paneled library. Its
carved wood shelves extending from ceiling to floor held gold-
embossed volumes of antique books as well as silver, brass and
porcelain treasurers collected by Lady Powell's family over many
generations. Clusters of photographs of the members of those
generations were discreetly displayed throughout the room.

Among the guests were a certain Major and Mrs. Edward
Drummond, perhaps the best known among the legendary families of Ireland. Edward owned stables, race horses, a golf course,
three hotels and an interest in the Bank of Ireland, among other
investments. His wife, Blanche, was not a particularly attractive

woman, somewhat dour, but well-educated, well-read, well-traveled, and ever ready to share her wealth of knowledge with anyone with a polite ear. At dinner, Milo, as guest of honor, was seated to the right of Lady Powell; in turn to his right he found Blanche Drummond. Surprisingly, her conversation was enlightening and clever and later Milo confided to his hostess that sitting next to Mrs. Drummond had been most enjoyable.

After dinner the party moved back to the drawing room where brandy and other cordials were served. Then came the special moment. All eyes were on the Prince as Lady Powell handed His Highness a small, beautifully wrapped box. Inside was a solid gold watch with chain and fob, his crest and initials engraved on the outside. Upon opening the case, he read, "From Doreen Powell, October 3, 1942".

The coming year found the two couples, Prince Milo and Lady Powell, Edward and Blanche Drummond sharing many social events together, luncheons, teas, and dinners at friends' homes, and of course, the races. On his birthday the following year, Milo received a sterling silver cigarette case, his crest and name "Milo" on the outside; inside it read, "With admiration, from your 'English Mother', Doreen Powell". January of the following year she died.

Milo and the Drummonds became three, Blanche right on hand to console His Highness in the loss of his dear friend. His dear friend had left much of her estate to the Prince, for which he was extremely grateful. As Major Drummond was considerably older than Milo, he already had started becoming less and less interested in social activities, while Blanche, on the other hand, herself twelve years Milo's senior, looked upon the tall, handsome Prince as the answer to all of life's unfulfilled expectations. The Prince's friendship with Mrs. Drummond continued, and grew—into a romance. Their clandestine meetings did not remain a secret; the love affair became a scandal, the shock of all of Dublin. When the Major threw her out, she went to live with the Prince. They became "the odd balls of their social class" as a close banker friend of both was wont to say.

In February of 1944, the V-1 rocket bombs hit England; it was the "Little Blitz" and 5,000 were killed; again in September, the V-2 rockets hit west London. Milo followed the war news by newspaper and radio, as well as occasionally catching some newsreels at the theatre. On October 20, in Yugoslavia, Tito's Partisan Army, pretty well known as pro-communistic, together with Russian troops, liberated Belgrade and Dubrovnik from the Nazis and the Fascists, and a half a year later, in April of 1945, they took Sarajevo back from the Axis. Across the Adriatic, in Milan, Benito Mussolini, no longer the swaggering Italian dictator, was shot and killed, along with his mistress, Clara Petacci, and together, strung up, upside down, in the Piazza Loreto, for all to see. The war in Europe was finally coming to an end; on May 8th, it was official, V-E Day. August 15th saw Japan surrender and V-J Day declared. Among the casualties of the war was the kingdom of Yugoslavia. The King of Serbia, who had become the King of Yugoslavia, because of all the internal rivalries and hatreds, lost his ill-gained kingdom to the Partisan Communists, as Marshall Tito became the country's first President.

Early in 1945 Milo announced to Mrs. Drummond that he had invited his sixteen year-old daughter in American to come visit him. Mrs. Drummond didn't know he had a daughter.

I tore open the letter postmarked Dublin, Eire, 12th May, 1945, and my eyes raced over the three small handwritten pages. It couldn't be.

The war in Europe was over. The trip had been arranged,

train and steamship reservations confirmed. Everything had fallen into place so perfectly.

The sentences leaped out from the pages, "It is all off. You cannot come to visit me. You do not love your Daddy. I shall not write you again."

The words blurred together. The chair was none too close as, with a swirling head, I reached for its arm and sank into it. I was weak and my fingers clutching the long-awaited letter limply fell open, letting it fall to the floor.

What had happened? Why this sudden change?

The late afternoon sun withdrew its light, and my happiness. I sat motionless in the darkening room? The dream of a lifetime had vanished, but why? I heard the sound of a key in the lock. That would be Mother. What would she think, what would she say? She would know what to do to make it all right. Yes, she would know.

Helena unlocked the door and entered to an almost dark room, I sitting in the corner, hunch-backed, head down, crying.

"My darling, what is it, what is wrong?"

"Oh, Mother, I can't believe it, this letter from Father. He doesn't want me. He never did; I know it. He's wiggling out of promises he never intended to keep."

Helena picked the letter up from the floor and read it.

"I can't believe he would write you like this. Me, yes, but why you? To make excuses he turns everything around."

"What do you mean?"

Helena took off her coat and laid it to one side as she sat down on the sofa beside her distraught daughter.

"Darling, I have tried never to talk against your Father. On the contrary, I have always tried to make everything sound all right, even when it wasn't. But I think I must let you know some things you have not known before.

"It was I who suggested the trip to him, that perhaps he would like to see you and at the same time offer you the opportunity of a trip to Europe as a graduation present from high school, before you go on to university. In recent letters he described his home and car, sent pictures of them, and has talked about his buying and selling antiques, and so I felt he must have some money now and would be able to do this, inasmuch as he hadn't done much of anything before. His letter that came back expressed great pleasure in the idea of seeing both of us again after all these years.

"A couple of months after this, after plans were in motion, he wrote to me saying I should not come, that you should come alone, that it would not look right if I were there. At first I thought okay, I understand. Then later I began to think that there was something more behind this change of attitude. Of course, he has another woman; after all these years it would be expected. He would have considered that when I first suggested the idea but he expressed pleasure in it. So what caused the change? I sensed he might be thinking about keeping you, not letting you return. I couldn't stand that, losing you at this point. I couldn't possibly afford an international legal battle to get you back. Something was wrong, somewhere. I wrote back telling him you could not come without my chaperoning you as I considered you too young to travel half way around the world without a chaperone. This letter to you is his answer. He shouldn't have written you like this; it is to me he should have written." Helena burst into uncontrollable sobs.

"Mother, I can't believe he would do that to me, keep me. I'm sure when I would tell him it was time for me to return he would let me go."

"You don't know him, darling. You were only eight months old when he left, promising we would all be reunited soon. That was fifteen years ago. I am the one who has brought you up, alone, with no help from him. I just couldn't stand losing you to him now, with your college life all set up ahead. For him to just take you away from me, I . . . I . . . "

I put my arms around my Mother and squeezed her tightly,

"I understand. I love you, Mother, and I wouldn't ever want for you to be hurt. It's okay."

There was enough hurt in that room that night to last both of us for a long time.

The charcoal gray Daimler wound its way along the low stone wall of the narrow road that leads out from Dublin. The ride to Galway County would take about three hours. A county of many contrasts, the western part, known as Connemara, has been described as more a state of mind and soul than a geographical location. Between Lough Corrib and the Atlantic Ocean, the narrow, winding roads are often lined with the bright color of fuchsia, the gleam of Connemara marble, and the rough texture of low stone fences. There is a quality of primitive quiet here that calms the spirit of even the most anxious. At first sight, travelers usually fall silent, a reverent response to the tranquility and splendor of the peaceful surroundings.

Nestled at the foot of the fog-shrouded Ben Lettery Mountain in Connemara is the Ballynahinch River, some three miles long, including Loughs Inagh and Derryclare as well as the Ballynahinch Lake. A privately-owned wild sea trout and salmon preserve, which, at the beginning of the century belonged to the Maharaja Ranjit Sinji, Milo and Blanche had been invited by the present owners to picnic and fish there anytime they wished. Arriving with wicker picnic hamper in hand, and full, they stopped by a pretty field of fresh green young shoots and late-spring purple heather ambling over the rolling terrain and the rocky ledges alongside the stream. Over yonder a fisherman in high shiny boots stood knee deep, his line out, waiting for the trout or salmon to take the bait, while a couple of sheep wandered over from the field close by to observe the action, or lack of it. After the throw was spread on the ground, the finest damask cloth on top, Milo and Blanche sat down to enjoy a feast of smoked salmon, pate, prawns, wine, cheese, fruit, and some fine, crusty bread, all on or with French crystal glasses, Wedgwood china, and Sheffield silver-plated flatware. All the better to enjoy, my dear.

"I think Mr. Allen is holding out for a higher price on the three paintings, but in vain. With the war and all, people don't have money to spare. He'll be out in three weeks with the paintings, and I'm sure he'll accept my offer," said Prince Milo, nodding to himself with great satisfaction.

"Yes, and with that we will have all the walls of two houses filled with paintings. Have you decided which ones you are thinking of selling this time?" inquired Blanche in her usual vaguely sullen demeanor. "We're running out of space."

"I'll see which ones catch his eye and take it from there. There are a couple he mentioned six months or so ago, and, of course, my portrait, which he's always after and which I shall not release to him under any circumstances. He says he wants it only for display in his studio, but, that means some offers as lead-ins. No, he shall not get his hands on that."

"Um-hum, good. And Milena, how are plans going for her visit?"

"Helena placed some conditions on the trip that I couldn't agree to, so the plans are off."

That was that. Taciturn was the word to describe the Prince. One did not question too far. Even if one did it would be useless; there would be no answer. To be truthful, she wasn't particularly anxious for his only child to come into his life after all these years. She, herself, had been an only child and was now alienated from her own daughter. She had disinherited her just as she herself had been disinherited by Major Drummond, even though they were still legally married. Milo and his wife had divorced after ten years of separation, but both were unmarried. This was of concern to Blanche. No, she did not want Helena nor Milena on the scene. His answer pleased her.

They picked up their picnic things and continued their drive through the unpolluted land of ancient Celts, poets and writers, to their two-hundred year old thatched-roof cottage in the Errisbeg mountains overlooking the rugged Atlantic coastline.

HOM

8 | The Prodigal Father

The flames in the fireplace leaped up to form dancing, shadowy figures on the walls, then quickly fell back down again to play amongst the smoldering embers. It was December; at three in the afternoon, it was dark outside in this land of the midnight sun. Come summer, things would be reversed; there would be daylight for nineteen or twenty of the twenty-four hours.

It had been this way every afternoon since I arrived at Errisbeg. We would sojourn to the den after the mid-day meal, which was the main meal of the day. Father would stoke the fireplace and we'd sit down in the two overstuffed chairs, quietly watching the flames shoot up and cast their glow and warmth throughout the small room, crowded with the two chairs, a small table between, a desk and chair and some bookcases against the walls. Some time would pass before there would be any conversation. Eventually a comment or a question would lead into a continuation of my Father's life story.

Arranmore Road had been home to my Father and Mrs. Drummond for over ten years. The 200 year-old thatched-roof cottage at Connemara had been at first a country home, a place to get-away from the city for a couple of weeks, or for vacation during two or three months in the summer. As the years passed, they found themselves spending more and more time there, until one day they decided to sell the Dublin house and move permanently to Connemara. It was like Montenegro; time and the winds of change had not made a mark on the rugged, stone hills. People valued this barren and seemingly hostile place, attested to by the very existence of the long, carefully made stone walls that separated each rocky field from its neighbor, running in lines up and over hills where the sheep roamed in uninterrupted serenity. The stones of the walls were spaced somewhat apart so that the winds that swept across the open, treeless plateaus could continue unimpeded on their journey.

On the nine-acre parcel in front of the cottage, Milo had built a larger house where I was now visiting and had as my guest quarters the room that used to be Mrs. Drummond's. Father still maintained his activity in buying and selling paintings, furniture, objects d 'art, and gold coins, as the stacks of catalogues from Sotheby's and Christie's lining the walls of the living room and den attested to. Representatives from the London and Dublin antique shops and auction houses made regular trips out to Errisbeg to see what the reclusive Prince had decided to sell. He no longer took trips away from home, so his purchases he now made solely from catalogues. Luckily, this was during a thirty-year period of ever increasing value of collectibles.

In the mid 1960s, Mrs. Drummond died. Now alone in this remote, isolated spot on the Atlantic coast in Co. Galway, at a half-way point on the road that wound along the stark, stunning stretch from Roundstone to Clifden, the reclusive life he had led in the immediately previous years continued on uninterrupted. He sold his Daimler as he was no longer driving. The postal carrier took his grocery list one day and delivered his groceries back the next along with his mail. Tom, his man-servant, came in daily for a few hours to take care of the place, and to handle the turf and logs used for burning in the fireplaces and in the Aga stove in the kitchen. Father could not have survived without him, and even though there were times he, justifiably, was ready to walk out on Father, he was with him to the end.

Mr. Reginald Miley, a retired banker from the Bank of Ireland, was Father's one friend. A good friend he was; and he became a good friend to me, also. I never will forget my first day

My Father, The Prince

there. He arrived, unannounced, to visit Father; it had to be unannounced because Father's phone seldom worked. Father expected him, however, once every two or three weeks, whenever he came out to his country place just up the road for a few days. He took care of Father's business needs, as well as any other little thing that came up that Father needed help in handling. For one thing, Father could be quite difficult and was suspicious of everyone. Not of Mr. Miley, nor of me, thank goodness; but Mr. Miley was often needed to step in on little matters in Father's behalf and smoothen things out.

Soon after being introduced that day to Regie and chatting a bit, we found ourselves alone.

"You know, up until ten minutes ago I didn't even know you existed!

I withheld a gasp.

He continued, "I'm glad you do. I don't know what brought you here now, but the timing is good. I don't know if you know about the lady, but—"

"Yes, I do, Mrs. Drummond."

"Right. She died only about a half a year ago."

"That I didn't realize," I said.

"He needs someone now. He has made himself into a recluse, made it clear to anyone who dares come to the door that he doesn't want to see them and orders them off his property. Nobody likes him because he is so unfriendly. Put himself right into a bind he has. How long are you going to stay?"

"Not very long," I replied. "I have a husband and a career. I am not able to be here for long stretches, but I hope to come and see him maybe a couple of times a year, if he'll have me. It's been almost forty years . . . he left when I was eight months old, so this is the first time I've met my Father. My Mother brought me up. And may I add, she was a wonderful person. She is dead now."

"I'm sorry." Regie gave a soft smile, and I felt right off he had taken a liking to me, "I didn't know he had been married; I

160

admit I had wondered about it, but he never mentioned anything. I'm very glad you're here. I think you're probably the best thing he ever did!"

Father's two dogs came up and nuzzled us, one an elegant black and white Dalmatian and the other a golden Retriever. They knew Regie and even though I had been there less than twenty-four hours, they already understood I belonged there.

"Do you remember when you were going to come and visit me, oh, that was over twenty years ago?", my Father asked right out of the blue, after we had settled down for the afternoon's chat.

"Yes," I replied and said no more.

"Well, your Mother scotched that deal. I want you to know that had you come I would have kept you here!"

I couldn't believe what I was hearing. My Mother was right. No more was ever said about that subject.

"I hope to visit Montenegro one day," I said during one of our fireside chats. He looked at me, surprised.

"I never went back," he replied brusquely, somehow, by implication, asking, why then would you go? "It's been fifty-five years. Well, you wouldn't mention me, it's a different type of government now."

"Yes, I know. But I'm sure you can understand my desire to see my Father's fatherland."

He nodded. I think on further thought he could.

About three or four miles past Clifden, along Galway Road heading inland toward Dublin, near a small fishing lake, was "Solitude", a horse riding and pony trekking center from which one could take rides to the mountains, valleys and to the old

Connemara marble quarry nearby. We accidentally discovered it and its proprietor, Joe O'Flaherty, on an afternoon's ride. A fascinating place and with an equally fascinating gentleman proprietor we had stumbled upon, my only sojourn ever out of the house with my Father.

The O'Flahertys possessed the territory on the east side of Lough Corrib up until the thirteenth century, when, under pressure from the Anglo-Norman penetration into Connaught, they moved west to the other side of the lake. O'Flahertys are more numerous in Co. Galway than anywhere else; even with the passage of time, they prefer their natural habitat to any other place. Over the centuries, the clan has produced a number of eminent writers and historians. Thus it was with Joe, who had lived in the United States and had been in the nightclub business in New York. His home was in Longford, right in the center of Ireland; but like my Father, the land of Connemara had reached out and sucked him in. I understood that; it had gotten to me, too.

"Solitude" is no longer. I'm glad I saw it when I did. It remains a part of the nostalgic memories of my times in lovely Eire. I later visited Joe and his beautiful wife, Norma, in their home in Longford, staying not far away for a few days at the New Castle Hotel which, at the time, they owned. Looking back on those days I can only savor every minute of a peaceful way of life I shall never experience again.

Then the bombshell burst, Father told me that my short visits were not restful to him, that if I couldn't stay for a long time not to bother to come again!

9 | An Illyrian Summer

American Airlines 747 had just touched down at the Frankfurt airport when it hit me, what I was doing and the circumstances under which I was doing it. My husband of twenty years had died only a couple of months before. Austrian-Hungarian born under the old Empire, he had been part of the Hungarian army in World War I, fighting "on the wrong side". We had taken a trip to Hungary last year, his first and only one back since immigrating to the United States many years ago and this year it was to be my turn to go to back to my roots, to Montenegro for the first time. Because of his passing, I was about to cancel, but at the last moment stopped myself. Why not go? If I didn't go now, I might never. Then, if perchance the day ever came that I should see my Father again, I would be able to tell him that I had visited his beloved homeland. That is, if I ever saw him again.

A quick change of planes to Jugoslovenski Aerotransport and we were off to Dubrovnik on the Dalmatian coast, just north of Montenegro. Going through passport control upon landing, the man in the booth gave me a second look after seeing the name in my passport; I used Petrovic-Njegoš as my middle name. But, passport and visa both in order, he passed me through without any ado.

I went to inquire about getting a bus to my destination, Sveti Stefan, a couple of hours down the coast. There was no public bus to there. I looked for a taxi; there were none. Same for a car rental. I boarded a bus headed into the center of the city and asked the driver to let me off at a travel agency. This he did. Seated right at the first desk as one entered was a pleasant lady who, luckily, spoke English and I explained my problem. She thought for a moment and then leaped up and ran to the door. I turned around to see a Montenegroturist bus loading outside. After talking briefly with the driver, she called to me.

"He said he'll take you."

"Right to Sveti Stefan?" I asked.

"Yes."

"How'll I return?"

Another brief consultation. "What day do you want to return?" I told her.

Further discussion and she looked back at me, "He's scheduled to be returning from a trip that very day and can bring you back, leaving Sveti Stefan at two in the afternoon."

"How wonderful." I exclaimed, heaving a sigh of relief. "How can I ever thank you?" I tried to do that by pressing the palm, but she refused. I asked her name and said I would report upon my return. I did.

I'm practically hitch-hiking I giggled to myself as I climbed aboard the bus; imagine, a Princess traveling in "her country" by bus! Actually it was the way I did much of my traveling in that country. Later on, when tour guides would talk about the Royal Family of Petrovic-Njegoš and the last queen, Milena, I would feel sort of special inside. I was Milena, not that one, but related to her and named after her. I never said anything to anyone about my background; Montenegro was a Communist country with strongman Marshal Tito as its leader and I don't think I would have been welcomed. Actually very little mention was ever made of the former royal family, either verbally or in writing. It would appear that most references to them had been purged from their books and whenever any reference was made, it was usually to Petar Petrovic-Njegoš II, the 19th century Prince-bishop, as being the South Slavs most famous poet. His royalty was sloughed over but his burial in a mausoleum atop Mt. Lovcen was pointed out endlessly.

"A bad land, but a heroic one," he had written. "Accursed but ours."

It was a beautiful day. The walled city of Dubrovnik, for centuries the capital of a tiny republic called Ragusa, its white stone glowing in sunlight or moonlight, was a veritable museum of 16th and 17th century architecture. Its numerous palaces, towers, squares, monuments, churches, and museums made the fortress town a natural for placement on UNESCO's official list of the world's cultural and natural heritages.

We were soon across the border into the Republic of Montenegro, one of six republics and two provinces that made up the country of Yugoslavia at that time. Sometimes referred to as the Montenegrin Littoral, the long, jagged Dalmatian coastline with its countless coves, bays, sandy and rocky beaches and numerous islands off-shore, combined with towering mountain chains running parallel to the coast, sometimes only a thousand feet or less inland, shaded by lush Mediterranean vegetation in the coastal areas and forests in the mountain areas, all under the silvery blue-white Adriatic sky, was a stunning sight to behold. The farther south one went, the more beautiful it became.

In ancient times, around 200 B.C., Illyrians held sway in this land, under rule of a queen named Teuta. Long after the Greeks had sailed up from Corinth and built their trading colonies along the coast, Roman expansionist activities brought them into the area. Queen Teuta fought long and hard to stave them off but she failed. As legend goes, she drowned herself rather than submit to them.

The first major town across the border was 600 year-old Herceg-Novi, sometimes referred to as the "rainiest spot in Europe" with about 333" a year. Its population of about 12,000 lives at the majestic entrance to the sloping shores of the fiord-like Bay of Kotor, surrounded by Venetian, Turkish and Spanish

HOM

fortifications, and centered with a resplendent park of over one hundred kinds of tropical and sub-tropical plants, a veritable flower spectacle throughout most of the year. The city of Kotor itself, its old preserved rampart encircling the town and watch tower which in centuries past was the guardian for all Montenegro, shelters picturesque squares and narrow, meandering streets that curl around the gulf's four indentations to the 13th century cathedral on the far side, situated at the third and dug into the mountainscape which forms the bay, mountains plunging straight down into the smooth surface of the water, two monastery islands sparkling like jewels right in the center. Beautiful villas reflecting the rich architecture of various epochs nestle amongst the coves and bays as waterfalls sprout out from the surrounding cliffs.

Then came Budva, one of the oldest settlements on the Adriatic Coast, dating back as far as the IV century B.C., with archaeological remains from Illyrian, Greek, Roman and Byzantine eras. Once an island, it is now linked to the mainland by causeways. Eight years later most of this priceless antiquity would be lost to a major earthquake.

Up ahead of us to the left was Milocer, a former summer royal palace turned into a luxury hotel, set back in a magnificent park on the curve of the bay, while to the right just beyond lay Sveti Stefan, once a fortified fishing village on a tiny off-shore island, now transformed into a first-class luxury hotel connected to the mainland by only a pedestrian walkway.

The five centuries old medieval hotel, its towers and ramparts and winding stone streets and narrow stairways up and down hillsides mixed chic boutiques and centuries-old churches right in with the eighty small stone houses that had made up the old fishing village but that, now remodeled, had become one hundred sixteen quaint, shuttered guest apartments, each differing from the rest in size, elevation, shape, interior design and view. Amenities included a restaurant, an expansive terrace, a terrace cafe, snack bars, a bar, casino, barber shop, beauty salon, boutiques and a theatre. This would be home for the next ten days. I had been led to believe it was the best Montenegro had to offer. Having traveled extensively, I quickly saw it matched the best of anything, anywhere, and surpassed most. This, then, became the first surprise of my trip to Montenegro, that such an majestic and beautiful country could have been so disregarded by so many of the Western nations as to allow it to lose its independence.

After a day or two resting to get rid of the jet-lag, I was ready for the journey from Kotor up to the old capital of Cetinje, an incredible ride along dazzlingly steep, mountainous slopes. George Bernard Shaw, visiting the area at age 73, is reported to have said, "I have heard that the road from Kotor to Cetinje is one of the most beautiful in the world and that is the reason I have come. I have not been disappointed."

The hour-long drive over the hair-raising old road up the Lovcen Pass that zigzags, twists and serpentines right up the face of the Black Mountain, making some twenty-five hairpin bends in all before coming out onto a landscape of hugh bleached white limestone rock boulders and karstic crags, takes you to a region that, according to legend, was formed when God dumped a sack of leftover rock on a piece of already barren wasteland. Looking out along the way, the view of the awe-inspiring Gulf of Kotor resembles the crater of a volcano. On the way to the old capital we passed through the village of Njegusi where my Father had been born, also the native village of that esteemed Prince-bishop poet. I wished I could have determined which house my Father was born in, but I couldn't.

Cetinje, the former capital of Montenegro, lies at the foot of Mt. Lovcen in the center of the Cetinje plateau. A provincial town, pastel and clean, with white houses on tree-lined streets and a large park in the center, it stands out in sharp contrast against the rocky peaks surrounding it. Its best buildings were once home to the many foreign embassies represented there. Built about one hundred and fifty years ago, the former palace is now the official museum, known by the locals as the Biljarda Castle, named after the billiards table brought up from the coast to the palace by mule in the late nineteenth century. But it is the old monastery, founded in 1484, an outpost of freedom and independence, that is the town's most historical site. It was destroyed several times, but always rebuilt, the last time in the 18th century under the reign of Petar I. Below the church arcades are the tombs of several members of the royal dynasty.

We had lunch at a hotel. I don't remember what I ate; I just sat looking out the large windows at the breathtaking vistas. Over to the side I saw a Montenegrin man riding the family donkey to market while his wife trotted along behind them carrying a huge bundle—all part of the old tradition in which the male lazed around during the intervals between battles while the female did most of the daily chores, both inside and outside the house. Changes come slowly in Montenegro.

The trip back wound its way south over an asphalt road through an area that was the scene of the fierce battle waged by the Montenegrins, under my Father's command, against the French and the Austrians in World War I. From Budva it was just a few miles back to Sveti Stefan.

A Montenegrin gentleman entered my life while I was there.

He was at Sveti Stefan almost daily and spoke English. I enjoyed having someone to talk to about Montenegro, how the government functioned, how the hotel was managed, how people lived. I also observed a lot; I read people, how they treat each other, their expressions, their attitudes, their mannerisms. Lack of mental stimulation and restriction of choices and opportunities stunts human development. The lovely people of this beautiful country deserved better.

One evening there was a reception at the island-hotel in honor of an artist who was displaying his paintings, sculpture, jewelry, etc. I attended it and spotted the gentleman. As we began talking another gentleman came up to speak to him and I moved away to examine some of the artist's work. When he was finished he returned to me.

"You know, you are a very fine lady," he said, "You know place!"

I could hardly contain a smile. Oh, I do, do I! "Thank you," I replied, acknowledging what he thought was a compliment . . . I thought of the woman with the heavy bundle walking behind the man riding the donkey.

We had fun together. He made a point of seeing me every day; quite frequently we lunched together when I wasn't out sight-seeing. We dined at Milocer across the causeway; I felt this must have taken two weeks of his salary. Late one afternoon we sat out on the beach as an evening storm blew in from Africa, bringing with it almost tropical weather. I had been swimming that day and wasn't worrying about the wind messing up my hair. I was completely relaxed. He was asking about my day, what I did, who was there. He told me he was jealous of the hours I wasn't with him. I laughed and said that I had already spent millions of hours not with him. "That was true but very sad," he replied. He took my hand and held it for a long time.

"I don't ever want to let it go. I don't ever want to let you go. Do you think you could ever live here? Or, if not here, maybe some other European country such as Germany or Italy?"

"Yes, I think I could. I don't know that it would be possible now."

"Oh, I understand," he replied, thinking I meant the recent demise of my husband. But that's not was I was thinking of.

"I am older than you. Our lives have been quite different."

"I know; I must try to catch up with you. I don't know if it is possible, but I would try. Would you give me a chance?"

"I don't think it is me who needs to give you the chance. I think it will be up to you."

"I love you. You're the first woman I've ever loved, and no matter what happens I will always love you."

I did not see him the morning I was to leave. As I was checking out at the front desk, he came up just as the reception clerk

HOM

handed my passport back to me, still opened to the identification page.

"You are Petrovic-Njegoš?"

"Yes, a distant relative", I replied, making light of it.

He was very quiet as he carried my suitcase across the causeway to the mainland where the bus driver had said he would pick me up at two o'clock.

"You're a Petrovic-Njegoš. And I said you knew place!" He shook his head and we both laughed.

We weren't very talkative; we smiled at each other as he held my hand, stroking it and turning it back and forth in his.

"I don't want this to be the last time I'll ever see you," he said.

"Nor do I."

Then the bus arrived to take me to Dubrovnik.

As the bus pulled away I waved out the window to him until a curve in the road took him from sight.

When we reached the Dubrovnik airport, the big Boeing 747 was already boarding passengers, and after clearance at the gate, I headed out across the tarmac. The theme song from the movie, "Dr. Zivago", floated through the air:

"Someday, we'll meet again I know, Someday, whenever the spring breaks through. You'll come to me, out of the long ago . . ."

I wondered if that really could ever be.

The engines were being warmed up as I put my tote up overhead and settled myself in my seat. I looked out the window. It couldn't be!

There on the other side of the fence was my new friend waving madly to me. He had no car. How did he get there? It didn't matter; he wanted to be there and somehow he did it.

I waved back until the plane took off and he was no more.

10 | An Old Soldier Fades Away

In 1977 I received a long-distance call from Ireland; it was Regie Miley. He said my Father was becoming quite frail and wanted to see me again but didn't have the nerve to ask me after having told me not to bother to come again unless I could remain for long periods of time. It wasn't restful to him . . . I remembered well the words he wrote. In the meantime, I had written to him of my husband's death; the main comment in his short reply was, "Well, that's life." That's true; it is. But I had hoped for something more, such as, "Maybe you'd like to get away. Why don't you come and visit your old Daddy on your next vacation?" That didn't happen, and six years passed until the day I received Regie's phone call. I left for Ireland two days later.

This time I chose to land at Dublin because there were a few things I wanted to buy to take out to Father, things he loved but couldn't buy locally and wouldn't ask anyone to send him, such as: Beluga caviar, pate de foie gras, some French cheeses, special biscuits for these items, and the like. I had sent him gift packets like this before, kiddingly referring to them as "Care Packages". Some years prior when I visited him, I brought him two gifts from fine men's shops in the United States, both of which I thought he would use a lot. Actually I was right, but it took him awhile to realize it. One was a brown velour shirt, his favorite color, along with a silk paisley scarf. He said the shirt wasn't warm enough for him in the cold Irish climate. I pointed out that he usually wore layers of clothing, and this would work nicely as almost any layer, whether for indoors or outdoors, with the scarf tucked around his neck. He always wore a cap, even indoors, not just for warmth but to hide the fact that he had become completely bald. (Obviously, he wasn't aware of what Yul Brunner had done for bald-headed men!) I thought the shirt and scarf, along with his cap, would make for quite a smart indoor outfit. He grunted a thank you, put the items in a bedroom drawer and there they remained for the remainder of my stay. The other item was a can opener, a much easier and more efficient one to use than the rusty, old-fashioned one he had. After I showed him how to use it, he put that in the kitchen drawer and there it remained for the remainder of my stay. When I tried to suggest that he try using it, he told me the one he had was best.

The drive from Dublin to Connemara passed "Solitude". It was still there, and out in the field was Joe riding one of his horses. I slowed down and gave a wave. He saw me and forthwith went into a gallop straight toward the car.

"How's the Princess?" he inquired as he swung down from his horse. "It's been a long time."

"I'm fine, but, unfortunately, Father is not. Yes, it has been a long time. A few years back Father decided if I couldn't stay for long stretches of time, really meaning all the time, he didn't want to bother with me. But just a couple of days ago, his good friend, Mr. Miley, rang me up to say that Father is going down hill rapidly and wants to see me but, at this point, was embarrassed to ask me. Here I am."

"That's great. While you're here, let me show you what I've done to "Solitude".

We walked to the house which had been remodeled into a shop, a charming tourist's boutique about native Ireland and the its products and customs. The problem was the location, like being at the end of the world; in the last hour of my drive I think I passed no more than half a dozen cars. Enchanting ideas conceived by exceptional people . . . if in life we could only catch them all.

I arrived at Father's in the mid-afternoon. Driving through the gates, I felt something was different; but I couldn't put my finger on it. As I took my suitcase out of the car and started up toward the house I realized what it was, the dogs hadn't run out to greet me. Reaching the foot of the stairs, I looked up and there at the top stood my Father, the Prince.

Our embrace told me he was as happy to see me as I was him. He was thinner and his "Montenegrin height" had shrunk; he moved more slowly, a bit stooped over.

"I don't climb the hills anymore," he said with his still impish grin.

My mind wandered back to my first visit. In the brisk wind of a mid-afternoon, we would walk up into the hills in back of his house. He'd be going like a mountain goat, his dogs yapping at his heels. I'd sit down on a large, flat boulder, and wait for him, letting the wind whip through my hair as I looked out over the angry Atlantic Ocean. Fate had finally caught up with herself and brought Father and Daughter together. Better late than never, I thought, even though I knew time was growing short. It was becoming very precious.

"Where are your dogs?" I asked, my mind returning to the present.

"I'll tell you all about them when we get inside."

He pointed to my room and I took my things in.

When I came out he was in the kitchen preparing afternoon tea, with a little glass of gin and sweet vermouth on the side. He liked a nice Port Salut cheese and put some on a Rosenthal china plate with a few Danish crackers on the side. Father had a flair in the kitchen; his omelettes were and remain to this day the very best I've ever had, and he could do a boiled beef or baked chicken dinner right along with the best of 'em.

"We sojourned to the study. The fire was crackling cozily

and bouncing its shadows off the wall just as it had some years before and we sat down to pick up where we had left off.

"Duke, the Dalmatian was run over by a car just up the road. It happened in the early morning before daylight. It was just awful; I don't know how she got out to the street. I was lucky Mr. Miley was here at the time. He knew about it before I, and he broke the news to me. He took care of all the details for me. You remember the Retriever, Missy? She was missing soon after that. They say she ran off to look for Duke, but I don't believe that's what happened. I think she was stolen. I think the first one was stolen, too, but she didn't cooperate and got run over in the process. They were both valuable dogs and after the first one was killed, whoever did it decided to come back and get the other."

I felt sorry for him, at his age and now totally alone in this remotest of places.

He asked when I had to go back, and I told him. I had taken time off from work; he said he understood. Our days together were peaceful, uneventful, and to me, beautiful. When I told him I had visited Montenegro and had gone to his birthplace, his eyes lit up and he smiled. We spent many hours reminiscing about Montenegro.

"I'm glad you went," he said, squeezing my hand. That was all I needed.

When I came out the next morning he was looking in some of his cabinets; he said he had a couple of things for me. He handed me the gold watch with his coat of arms on the cover and fob, and the silver cigarette case, both of which had been given to him by Lady Powell those many years ago; a medal from his uniform and his "working sword" (he had already donated his uniform and good sword to the Museum of Dublin before we met); and a collection of old, lace fans. As promised, some years prior he had sent me his life-sized portrait along with a couple of other antique paintings, all of which were now hanging on the walls of my home.

A few days later I realized he had worn the same shirt every day since I arrived, a sort of beige velour, with a silk scarf around his neck. Then it dawned on me, this was the very shirt and scarf I had given him years ago, now faded from wear and repeated washings. The next day I made it a point to go into the kitchen when I heard a can being opened. He was using the can opener I had given him, and with great facility, obviously having used it quite a bit. He saw me looking at it and smiled.

"I threw the old one out; it wasn't working any more."

When I left he seemed stronger, more agile, smiling more. More important, he seemed content with me. He said he didn't expect me to come back soon but that I was welcome anytime for any length of time. Now that I, too, was alone, I felt that in the future I would be able to come more often or stay longer. But it was too late.

I had not been home more than a couple of weeks when I received another call from Regie Miley. Soon after I left Father had become seriously ill and had taken to bed. Against his protestations, Mr. Miley had finally gotten a doctor into the house, a lady doctor, who "got Father's number" quickly and demonstrated a real knack for handling him. After a few days she told Regie death was imminent, within twenty-four to forty-eight hours. But he lingered on. She said she really didn't understand what was keeping him alive except she thought he hoped to see his daughter just one more time. Father had given them explicit instructions not to call me because I had been there so recently.

I took the plane for Ireland the next day. He had not moved from his bed in almost three weeks and by now could no longer speak. I sat by the side of his bed and held his hand in mine, that evening, the next day, and early the next evening, twenty-six hours after I had arrived, he died. The last of the old Montenegrin warriors was gone.

We buried him in the grounds of the Cathedral at Limerick, Regie and I. There were just the two of us, huddled together under one umbrella in a torrential rain, as they lowered the casket

OM

into the ground. Father had wanted to be buried in a mausoleum on a hilltop, just like the Poet Prince-Bishop Petar
Petrovic-Njegoš, but wasn't allowed. It didn't really matter,
though. For over half a century he'd had no home, and that is
where he really wanted to be.

Bibliography

Alexandrov, Victor, *THE END OF THE ROMANOVS*, Boston, Mass.: Little Brown & Co., 1966.

Burns, Edward McNall, *WESTERN CIVILIZATIONS, THEIR HISTORIES AND THEIR CULTURES*, New York, N. Y.: W. W. Norton and Company, Inc., 1958.

Ciubranovitch, Jovan, *THE GREATEST CRIME IN HISTORY*, London, England: Grant Richards, 1930.

Criscuolo, Luigi, *MONTENEGRO'S RIGHT TO LIVE*, New York, N. Y.: Charles H. Jones & Co., Inc., 1928.

Crankshaw, Edward, *THE FALL OF THE HOUSE OF HABSBURG"*, New York, N. Y.: Penguin Books, 1963.

Crow, John A., *ITALY, A JOURNEY THROUGH TIME*, New York, N. Y.: Harper & Row, 1956.

Dupuy, R. Ernest and Trevor N., *THE ENCYCLOPEDIA OF MILITARY HISTORY*. New York, N. Y.: Harper & Row, 1986.

Edmonds, Paul, *TO THE LAND OF THE EAGLE*, London, England: George Routledge & Sons, Ltd., 1927.

Fagyas, Maria, *DANCE OF THE ASSASSINS*, London, England: Weidenfeld and Nicolson, 1973.

Goralski, Robert, *WORLD WAR II ALMANAC, 1931–1945*, New York, N. Y.: Bonanza Books, 1981.

Gurney, Gene, *KINGDOMS OF EUROPE*, New York, N. Y., Crown Publishers, Inc., 1982.

Holmes, Richazrd, *THE WORLD ATLAS OF WARFARE*, New York, N. Y.: Viking Penguin Group, 1988.

HOM

Kelly, Lawrence, *ST. PETERSBURG*, New York, N. Y.: Atheneum, 1983.

Kinross, Lord, *THE OTTOMAN CENTURIES*, New York, N. Y.: Morrow Quill Paperbacks, 1977.

Kort, Michael, *THE SOVIET COLOSSUS*, New York, N. Y.: Charles Scribner's Sons, 1985.

Kubly, Herbert and the Editors of Time-Life Books, *ITALY*, New York, N. Y.: Time-Life Books, 1968.

Massie, Robert K., *NICHOLAS AND ALEXANDRA*, New York, N. Y.: Atheneum, 1976.

Massie, Robert K. and Jeffrey Finestone, *THE LAST COURTS OF EUROPE*, New York, N. Y.: The Vendome Press, 1981.

Milo, Prince of Montenegro, *THE INDEPENDENCE OF SMALL NATIONS AND THE EXTINCTION OF MONTENEGRO*, London, England: Hoyell, Watson & Viney, Ltd., 1930.

—————, *THE MONTENEGRIN MIRROR*, San Francisco, Ca.: Committee for Freedom and Independence of Montenegro, December 15, 1931.

Myles, Douglas, *RASPUTIN: SATYR, SAINT OR SATAN*, New York, N. Y.: McGraw Hill Publishing Co., 1990.

Nehru, Jawaharlal, *GLIMPSES OF WORLD HISTORY*, New York, N. Y.: The John Day Company, 1942.

Ometev, Boris and John Stuart, *ST. PETERSBURG, PORTRAIT OF AN IMPERIAL CITY*, New York, N. Y.: The Vendome Press, 1990.

Pauli, Hertha, *THE SECRET OF SARAJEVO*, New York, N. Y.: Appleton-Century, 1965.

Pelissier, Roger, *THE AWAKENING OF CHINA*, New York, N. Y.: G. P. Putnam's Sons, 1967.

Podenzani, Nino. *VILLA D'ESTE*, Cernobbio, Italy, Villa d'Este, 1965.

Popovitch, Major Marko Zekov, *WHERE IS MONTENEGRO*, London, England: 1926.

Procacci, Guiliano, *HISTORY OF THE ITALIAN PEOPLE*, New York, N.Y.: Harper & Row, 1968.

Quirk, Robert E., *Mexico*, Englewood Cliffs, N.J.: Prentice-Hall, Inc., 1971.

Rasputin, Maria and Patti Barham, *Rasputin, The Man Behind the Myth*, Englewood Cliffs, New Jersey: Prentice-Hall, 1977.

Raymond, Ellsworth and John Stuart Martin, *A Picture History of Eastern Europe*, New York, N.Y.: Crown Publishers, Inc. 1971.

Resnick, Abraham, *Russia, A History to 1917*, Chicago, Illinois: Children's Press, 1983.

Ryan, Philip, *Pathways of Peter, the Great*, London, England: AHI International, 1989.

Salisbury, Harrison E., *Black Night, White Snow: Russia's Revolutions 1905—1917*, Garden City, New York: Doubleday & Company, Inc., 1977.

Seagrave, Sterling, *The Soong Dynasty*, New York, N.Y.: Harper & Row, 1985.

Stevenson, Francis Seymour, *A History of Montenegro*, London, England: Jarrold & Sons, 1912.

Stillman, Edmund and the Editors of Time-Life Books, *The Balkans*, New York, N.Y.: Time, Inc., 1964.

Taylor, A.J.P., *The Last of Old Europe*, New York, N.Y.: Quadrangle, The New York Times Book Company, 1976.

Walters, E. Garrison, *The Other Europe: Eastern Europe to 1945*, New York, N.Y.: Dorset Press, 1990.

Wells, H.G., *The Outline of History*, Garden City, N.Y.: Garden City Publishing Co., 1920.

Wolfson, Victor, *The Mayerling Murder*, Englewood Cliffs, N.J.: Prentice Hall, Inc., 1969.

Wright, William, "Leningrad", *Travel and Leisure*, 1989, pp.130–140, 154–155.

Wyon, Reginald and Gerald Prance, *The Land of the Black Mountain*, London, England: Methuen & Co., 1903.

OM

Notes and Sources

Title Page, Preface and Chapter One, To the Emerald Isle.

1. The literal translation of the name Petrovic-Njegoš from the Serbo-Croatian language which uses the Cyrillic alphabet to the English language which uses the Roman alphabet is Petrovic-Njegoš, Niegos, Njegus, or Niegush. To give the English-speaking world an easier, more phonetic spelling, the name has been spelled Petrovich-Niegosh, Petrovitch-Niegosch, or Niegoch, or Niegoche.

Chapter Two, Montenegro.

1. Sources of information regarding the Austrian-Hungarian Empire and the Imperial House of Habsburgs included *The Secret of Sarajevo*, *The Mayerling Murder*, *The Fall of the House of Habsburg*, *A History of the Habsburg Empire*, *The Last Courts of Europe*, *Kingdoms of Europe*, as well as reminiscences of my Father, H.H. Prince Milo of Montenegro, and those of the late Nicholas Winckler, a native of Austria-Hungary, and some of his family and friends who lived there during the latter part of that period.

2. Serbia and its two royal dynasties have received author research from *The Last Courts of Europe*, *The Secret of Sarajevo*, *Kingdoms of Europe*, *Dance of the Assassins*, *A Picture History of Eastern Europe*, *The Other Europe: Eastern Europe to 1945*, and other sources.

3. Information regarding Montenegro, its history and customs, and members of the royal dynasty of Petrovic-Njegoš was based upon my Father's reminiscences, as well as information derived from The Geneological Table of the Royal House of Petrovic-Njegoš, a number of newspaper clippings from the 1920s and early 1930s, and three books on Montenegro published in the early 1900s, *A History of Montenegro*, *The Land of the Black Mountain* and *To the Land of the Eagle*.

Chapter Three. St. Petersburg.

1. Three scholarly works have not only been helpful but fascinating in assisting to recreate life in early 20th Century St. Petersburg, namely: *Black Night, White Snow, Nicholas and Alexandra* and *St. Petersburg, Portrait of an Imperial City*.

2. My Father's reminiscences continue.

Chapter Four. A Russia Odyssey.

1. The three literary sources mentioned under Chapter Three continued to be most valuable, along with *Glimpses of World History*, *The Soviet Colossus*, *The Last Courts of Europe*, *Kingdoms of Europe*, *Russia, a History to 1917*, *St. Petersburg* and *Pathways of Peter, the Great*.

2. My Father's reminiscences.

3. Erudition about Gregori Rasputin was enhanced by *RASPUTIN, the Man Behind the Myth* and *Rasputin, Satyr, Saint or Satan*, as well as by the source material about Russia listed under Chapter Three.

Chapter Five. Montenegro Betrayed.

1. My Father's reminiscences.

2. Certain events surrounding World War I and its battles were partially reconstructed from *The Encyclopedia of Military History*, *The World Atlas of Warfare*, *Western Civilizations, Their History and Their Culture*, *The Outline of History* and *Glimpses of World History*.

3. Much of the material relating to Montenegro's role in World War I and its subsequent betrayal by some of its allies was derived from five limited-edition publications, *The Independence of Small Nations and the Extinction of Montenegro*, *The Greatest Crime in History*, *Montenegro's Right to Live*, *Where is Montenegro?* and *The Montenegrin Mirror*.

4. The terrifying end of the Romanovs has been copiously reported in a number of historical works, including *The Romanovs*, as well as in the first two books mentioned under Chapter Three.

Chapter Six. A Prince Without a Country.

1. Numerous newspaper articles from the 1920s through the 1950s proved helpful in recreating aspects of my Father's days in Italy, as well as personal notes taken during the author's visits there.

2. The Villa d'Este published a charming book about itself in 1965 which recounts its historical background and adds to the enchantment of one of the favorite places of both the subject and the author.

3. *Italy, A Journey Through Time*, *A History of the Italian People*, *Mexico*, *The Awakening of China* and *The Soong Dynasty* set forth background data relative to my Father's time in those countries.

4. My Father's reminiscences.

Chapter Seven. A New Life.

1. Both my Father's and my Mother's reminiscences were a major basis for this chapter.

2. Newspaper clippings of the late 1920s and the 1930s and 40s were helpful, as well as three books on military maneuvers, *The Encyclopedia of Military History*, *The World Atlas of Warfare* and *World War II Almanac, 1931-1945*. The five Montenegrin publications listed under Chapter Five provided further little-known but significant facts.

3. My reminiscences.

Chapters Eight, Nine and Ten.

1. My Father's and my reminiscences.

Index

ЧОМ

OM

ЮM

ЭM

Printed in the United States
3825